PENGUIN CLASSICS

THE FIRST POEMS IN ENGLISH

MICHAEL ALEXANDER's verse translations from Old English in-
clude *The Earliest English Poems* (1966) and *Beowulf* (1973),
both in Penguin Classics, and *Old English Riddles from the Exeter
Book* (Anvil Press, 1980, 2007). Other publications are Penguin
editions of *Beowulf* and of Chaucer, a study of Ezra Pound, and
a well-liked *History of English Literature* (Palgrave, 2000, 2007).
He has retired from the Chair of English Literature at the Univer-
sity of St Andrews and lives at Wells in Somerset. His most recent
publication is *Medievalism: The Middle Ages in Modern England*
(Yale University Press, 2007).

T0200775

The First Poems in English

Translated and edited by
MICHAEL ALEXANDER

PENGUIN BOOKS

PENGUIN CLASSICS

Published by the Penguin Group
Penguin Books Ltd, 80 Strand, London WC2R 0RL, England
Penguin Group (USA) Inc., 375 Hudson Street, New York, New York 10014, USA
Penguin Group (Canada), 90 Eglinton Avenue East, Suite 700, Toronto, Ontario, Canada M4P 2Y3
(a division of Pearson Penguin Canada Inc.)
Penguin Ireland, 25 St Stephen's Green, Dublin 2, Ireland
(a division of Penguin Books Ltd)
Penguin Group (Australia), 250 Camberwell Road, Camberwell, Victoria 3124, Australia
(a division of Pearson Australia Group Pty Ltd)
Penguin Books India Pvt Ltd, 11 Community Centre, Panchsheel Park, New Delhi – 110 017, India
Penguin Group (NZ), 67 Apollo Drive, Rosedale, North Shore 0632, New Zealand
(a division of Pearson New Zealand Ltd)
Penguin Books (South Africa) (Pty) Ltd, 24 Sturdee Avenue, Rosebank, Johannesburg 2196, South Africa

Penguin Books Ltd, Registered Offices: 80 Strand, London WC2R 0RL, England

www.penguin.com

Translations first published 1966; revised and expanded 1991
This edition first published in Penguin Classics 2008

019

Copyright © Michael Alexander, 1966, 1977, 1991, 2008
All rights reserved

Some of the Riddles originally appeared in *Old English Riddles from the Exeter Book* (translated by Michael Alexander), published by the Anvil Press, 1980

The moral right of the translator and editor has been asserted

Set in 10.25/12.25 pt PostScript Adobe Sabon
Typeset by Rowland Phototypesetting Ltd, Bury St Edmunds, Suffolk
Printed and bound in Great Britain by Clays Ltd, Elcograf S.p.A.

ISBN: 978-0-140-43378-4

www.greenpenguin.co.uk

For Lucy, Patrick and Flora

Contents

Preface

Most of the verse translations in *The First Poems in English* first appeared in book form in 1966, in a Penguin Classics edition entitled *The Earliest English Poems*. This anthology contained a selection of the shorter Old English poems, with four passages from *Beowulf*. These were prefaced by a general introduction, and each poem or group of poems also had an introduction, with notes at the end of the book and suggestions for further reading. *The Earliest English Poems* stayed in print, and subsequent editions in 1977 and 1991 included several new translations, various minor changes to the introductory sections, and an updated Further Reading. The time has now come to rewrite the book afresh.

The introductions, headnotes to the poems and other editorial material in the present book are new, but the verse translations are largely unchanged. These translations have met with a surprising success, appearing in anthologies made by the poets W. H. Auden, D. J. Enright, Charles Tomlinson, Donald Davie, Ted Hughes, Seamus Heaney and Paul Muldoon. They have been published in school and college anthologies, broadcast and set to music by composers, and even won the translator awards of some monetary value. They led Betty Radice of Penguin Classics to commission a translation of *Beowulf* and Peter Jay to commission translations of a much larger selection, *Old English Riddles from the Exeter Book*, for his Anvil Press. All these verse translations have gone into further editions and have not gone out of print. In their various forms they must between them have sold a million copies, striking testimony to the perennial appeal of these poems.

I hope that the translations remain fresh. They were produced in the belief that the best literature of the past remains current. The new editorial material in the book is informed by greater knowledge of Old English texts and their contexts. Yet it is designed, as before, to reach the widest possible audience.

Introduction

More manuscript poetry survives in English from before the Norman Conquest than in any other vernacular language in Europe. About 31,000 lines of verse survive, mostly in four manuscripts written about the year AD 1000.

In his *History of the English Church and People*, completed in 731, Bede wrote that the best English poet was the first, the seventh-century cowman Cædmon. King Alfred, however, thought that the best of the poets who had composed in English had been Aldhelm, Abbot of Malmesbury and Bishop of Sherborne, who died in 709.

That a king who died in 899 should have opinions about the merits of an English poet of the seventh century should disturb the popular notion that Geoffrey Chaucer, who died in 1400, was the Father of English poetry. Chaucer collected this compliment from John Dryden, in his Preface to the *Fables* (1700). Dryden's salute, made almost in passing, echoes those made by a series of Chaucer's successors and imitators, from Thomas Hoccleve down to John Milton. Chaucer had developed the verse line consisting of five metrical 'feet' which became the metre of much classical English poetry. Yet to install him as the originator of all English poetry is to ignore native traditions of alliterative verse which preceded literacy, and remained popular long after Chaucer's day. Contemporary poets in the alliterative tradition included the anonymous author of *Sir Gawain and the Green Knight* and the William Langland who composed *Piers Plowman*. Dryden had not read these poems, which were not in print. Unfamiliar with Old English, he would, like nearly all his contemporaries, have been quite unable to read the English manuscript verse surviving from before the Norman Conquest.

Chaucer is indeed the first writer in English to have been read with pleasure in every generation since his death. Literary merit plays its full part in this distinction, yet Chaucer was fortunate in being born in London in the early 1340s. His literary quality is seen in such lines from *The Canterbury Tales* as 'A sheaf of peacock arrows, bright and keen' (from the description of the Yeoman in the General Prologue) and 'The smiler with the knife under the cloak' (from the description of the Temple of Mars in the Knight's Tale). They are well turned and run in a rhythm now familiar. But they also read easily because they are in London English and because modern English descends from London English, though of a slightly later complexion. If Chaucer helped to found the modern tradition, English verse was already ancient. The English of William Langland, who came from Malvern in Worcestershire and wrote in the dialect of the West Midlands, is much more unfamiliar than Chaucer's. And if we go back to the English of King Alfred, we find that we cannot read it without first studying it.

Yet the language of Alfred is still English. Historians of the language call it Old English, but it is English all the same. Historians of the language classify the English of Chaucer's day as Middle English. 'Old English' designates the English spoken before 1100, a Germanic tongue untouched by French. 'Middle English' applies to the various (Frenchified) forms of the language used between *c.*1100 and *c.*1470. What we have been speaking since about 1470 is termed 'Modern English'. The early form of the language, before it was reclassified as Old English, was known as 'Anglo-Saxon'. Before that it was 'Early English' or 'Saxon' or 'semi-Saxon', and had other names. Scholars now confine 'Anglo-Saxon' to the people of between 450 and 1066 in what became England. 'Old English' is now the name for the language. Technical terms have their place and their use, yet a deeper point is in danger of being lost here: the language used by Cædmon, Aldhelm, Bede and Alfred is English. Some early English writing – Alfred's, for example – also reflects the kind of practical common sense which has often been considered typically English. To call it 'Anglo-Saxon' denies its connection with later eras and with the present.

'Anglo-Saxon' is a term first found in the English translation, published in 1607, of William Camden's Latin work *Britannia*. The Latin designation *Angli Saxones* is much older, and seems first to have been used by Paul the Deacon, an eighth-century Lombard historian, who wished to distinguish the Saxons of England from the Old Saxons of continental Saxony. 'Anglo-Saxon' does not distinguish between the Angles and the Saxons who conquered Britain; nor does it seek to join them together. In fact, it is clear from Bede's *History* that Angles and Saxons thought of themselves as forming a *gens Anglorum*, a single people. The Welsh, Cornish and Bretons, and the Gaels of Ireland and Scotland, call the invaders 'Saxons'. Alfred was a Saxon, and Bede an Angle, but for both of these reflective men the Saxons south of the Thames Valley and the Angles to its north shared a *gens*: they belonged to the same family and shared an identity both ethnic and religious. Ecclesiastical unity came to Angles and Saxons in the seventh century, political unity in the tenth, when Mercia and then Northumbria accepted the rule of Wessex. This united country, at first *Engla-land* then *England*, was ruled by a Saxon dynasty.

The Modern English of today differs from Old English perhaps as much as modern French differs from the spoken Latin of late antiquity. But Old English is a simple language; it has only two tenses, a present and a past, and its grammar and accidence offer few difficulties to a linguist. Its prose is straightforward. But to the English reader who knows no other language, Old English looks very unlike the English spoken today. Yet the sentence 'Old English looks very unlike the English spoken today' contains only one word not found in Old English: the word 'very' from the French *vrai*. The basic components of Modern English are inherited from Old English. Yet the spellings of words, and the words themselves, changed so much after the Norman Conquest that the simplest Old English takes a little getting used to before it can be read and understood. Middle English was gradually colonized by thousands of French

words, and its structure and sounds also changed in deeper
ways. Most forms of words lost their endings, which obliged
the inter-relationships of words in a sentence to assume more
restricted patterns. English reached a recognizably modern
form at about the time that William Caxton brought a printing
press to London in 1476, and began to print Chaucer and
Malory and other English authors.

A number of books have been published with the title *The
Triumph of English*, one of them adding the dates '1350–1400',
1400 being memorable to those who know a little literary
history as the year of Chaucer's death. Those less acquainted
with literary history perhaps think of English literature as begin-
ning with Shakespeare. One-volume histories of England move
rapidly to Henry VIII, and one-volume histories of English
literature reach Shakespeare as fast as they can. But England
precedes Henry VIII, and its literature precedes Shakespeare.
Indeed, literature in English precedes the political unification
of England. *Beowulf* was composed before English achieved a
standard written form in the tenth century, when kings of
Wessex had become kings of England. English verse drama
reached a high point in the thirteenth century and was popular
and communal in character. It has already been noted that
Chaucer's contemporaries included several notable poets, such
as John Gower, Langland, and the author of *Sir Gawain and the
Green Knight*, who also wrote *Pearl*. Prose in English reached a
fine standard in the fifteenth century with Dame Juliana of
Norwich and Sir Thomas Malory. It can be seen, therefore, that
the components of modern English literature long precede the
Elizabethan period.

Writers in medieval times are normally modest about their
achievements, especially vernacular writers. The Renaissance
writer, by contrast, often blows the trumpet for his own lan-
guage, his country and himself. This prospectus for Renaissance
vernacular literature is still widely believed. Printing had greatly
increased the opportunities for self-publicists, and for govern-
ments. The habit of praising Tudor achievements, begun by
servants of the Tudors, has left English people misinformed
about earlier periods. Many people seem to believe that the

Bible was first translated into English during the Reformation. Yet Bede completed an English version of St John's Gospel eight centuries before that, in 735. We have a full translation of the four Gospels into idiomatic Old English in about the year 1000. King Alfred translated the Psalms, and Aelfric of Eynsham (c.955–1010) translated the book of Genesis. Another popular idea about medieval English religion is that it was conducted in Latin. Yet the English could scarcely have been converted in the seventh century had missionaries not told them of the Christian story in the local tongue. Homilies explaining the Scriptures survive by the hundred in Old English, by the thousand in Middle English.

These misconceptions about when English was first used for literary or religious purposes show the persistence in popular memory of partisan perspectives created at the time of the Reformation and cemented during the Enlightenment. The very terms 'the Anglo-Saxons' and 'Old English' perpetuate such perspectives, helping to make pre-Reformation England seem more distant and less English. But it needs to be remembered that there was an Archbishop of Canterbury before 600 and that King Edgar was crowned King of England in 973, in a rite which still forms part of the ceremony used on such occasions.

The writings of 'the Anglo-Saxons' were first reinvestigated under Queen Elizabeth I. Her Archbishop of Canterbury, Matthew Parker, was looking for evidence that English Christianity had been independent of Rome. Supporters of Parliament against the Stuarts sought evidence of primitive democracy in Anglo-Saxon England. A different expectation is displayed in Hippolyte Taine's *Histoire de la littérature anglaise* of 1863. In the pages of Taine, *les Anglo-Saxons* are large, beef-witted, hut-dwelling warriors awaiting the civilizing mission of Guillaume le Conquérant. Taine, a Positivist, was heir to the prejudices of the Enlightenment, prejudices once widely held in England. Indeed Alexander Pope, a Catholic who expressed conventional Enlightenment views, knew so little about the Middle Ages that he could write, in an historical survey towards the end of his *Essay in Criticism*: 'A Second Deluge Learning

thus o'errun, / And the Monks finished what the Goths begun.'
This is almost the opposite of what actually happened, certainly
in England.

Taine assumed that history showed progress, which it can.
But literary history, generally speaking, does not simply pro-
gress. Greek literature has not improved on Homer. Italian
literature has not improved on Dante. European drama has not
improved on Shakespeare. Taine also assumed that an oral
tradition would be crude. By contrast, those who know *Beowulf*
acknowledge its metrical skill, the quality of its language and
its sober grasp of some of life's fundamentals. Like Alexander
Pope, Taine further assumed that the literary skills of monks
would be rudimentary. Monks had a bad press after the Revol-
ution in France, as they had after the Reformation in England.
But medieval monks were literate, for literacy unlocked Scrip-
ture, and some monks were learned when no one else was
learned. Without the monks of the early Middle Ages, learning
would have disappeared from Western Europe. England,
indeed, has a unique debt to monasticism, because the forty
men sent by Pope Gregory I to evangelize the Angles came from
his own monastery on the Caelian Hill. This was Rome's first
mission, and the papacy backed it for generations, sending the
Cantor of St Peter's to show how the liturgy should be sung,
and staffing the monastic school at Canterbury with men of
literary ability. The superb monastic library collected by the
Anglian nobleman Benedict Biscop on his six trips to Rome
from northern England laid the foundation for Bede's learning.
The crucial point to grasp, in accounting for the creation of
Old English literature, is that both traditions, the vernacular
and the Latin, were in a flourishing state in seventh-century Eng-
land. Bede's story of the illiterate Cædmon composing a song of
the Creation celebrates precisely the fusion of the oral and the
literary, and the cultural energy which this fusion created.

After 1066, however, English was no longer the language of
the rulers. It remained the speech of the people, but local dialects
diverged more and more from each other. The practice of writ-
ing English in the standardized form it had reached in Wessex
of the tenth century was kept up in a few religious houses. The

monks of Medehamstead (modern Peterborough) continued their version of the *Anglo-Saxon Chronicle* until 1154, but manuscripts in the old language gradually lost their readers. An inventory of the library at Exeter Cathedral carried out in 1327 ends with 'many other books in French, English and Latin, worn out by age', which are described as 'worthless'. One of these was a book left to the cathedral by Leofric, the first Bishop of Exeter, who died in 1072. One of Leofric's legacies is *i.micel.englisc.boc.be.gehwilcum.thingum. on.leothwisan.geworht*: 'One large English book on various subjects, composed in verse form'. This manuscript, known as the Exeter Book, was written in about 970. The anthology contains nearly all of the shorter poems in Old English that modern readers have found attractive. The Exeter Book shows cuts, beer stains and burn marks, and has been robbed of some of its leaves. Presumably it was one of the old and 'worthless' books from the inventory of 1327, but it was the bequest of the first bishop and remained in the library of his cathedral. It was not until the 1360s that English replaced French as the language of Parliament, three centuries after the Norman Conquest. Geoffrey Chaucer began to write in the next decade. Three reigns later, Henry V spoke English in preference to French, the first English king to do so since 1066.

The earliest verse in English was not written but composed and recited aloud: chanted or sung by poets who could not write; the Old English word for 'poet' was *scop*, from *scieppan*, the word for 'to shape' or 'make'. Literacy was clerical, and Latin had what literary prestige there was. The Roman missionaries landed on the Isle of Thanet in 597, which is also the year in which St Columba died on the island of Iona. Within a few years, a Kentish law code was recorded in the English language, in a Latin alphabet and script. The conversion of these Teutonic pagans required the Gospels to be translated from the international into the local tongue. The early leaders of the Church in England included learned men, notably Theodore, who was Archbishop of Canterbury from 666 to 690. Theodore was a Greek, born near Tarsus. Another is Bede, the only Englishman writing before Geoffrey Chaucer to have found a general

readership in every succeeding generation. Bede, who wrote in
Latin though he could and did compose aloud in English, was
a monk at Monkwearmouth, a monastery founded by Benedict
Biscop in 674. Bede was chiefly a biblical commentator, but his
work best known to posterity is his history of the English
nation, *Historia ecclesiastica gentis Anglorum*.

The authority of Bede's learning established throughout
Western Europe his own practice of dating events from the
year of Christ's birth. Bede's reputation lasted long; he is, for
instance, the only Englishman mentioned in Dante's *Divine
Comedy*. Esteem for the learning of Northumbria (England
north of the Humber) was such that Charlemagne, crowned
emperor in 800, made Alcuin of York the master of his school.
But by the time of King Alfred (d. 899), the Latin literacy of
Bede's day had fallen away so completely that the king decided
to have what he called 'the books most necessary for all men
to know' translated into English. This was done, and a chronicle
was begun in West Saxon, the language of Wessex. Alfred also
tried to make provision for the free-born sons of the laity to
learn to read, and to read English. This did not have much
immediate success. Yet Alfred had instituted a programme for
writing in the vernacular, for lay people as well as the clergy,
in Wessex and in Mercia. This eventually had major conse-
quences: vernacular verse and prose began to appear, original
compositions as well as translations.

Monastic learning revived in southern England in the late
tenth century. Among the many surviving manuscripts are the
four major books of vernacular verse, written between 970 and
1030. As stated earlier, the total number of lines of verse to
survive is about 31,000. Prose survives in far greater quantity.
The extant verse must be a fraction of what there once was,
but 31,000 lines is quite a lot. Homer's *Iliad* has 15,700 lines,
Spenser's *The Faerie Queene* has 33,000 lines. Old English
verse is written continuously, as we write prose, reaching to the
edge of the page, for space was expensive. The production of
vellum cost a lot of labour (a book was made with the skins of
many calves). The Old English poetic texts, translated into
prose, fill a printed book of more than five hundred pages.[1]

This poetic corpus, predominantly religious in character, is both varied and interesting. Some of the shorter English poems have an excellence which survives translation and have thereby reached a public far greater than the more limited if still considerable number of people who have studied the original texts. I am thinking of *The Wanderer* and *The Seafarer*, for example, and the visionary poem known as *The Dream of the Rood*. (The titles are supplied by modern editors.) The epic *Beowulf* accounts for one tenth of the lines that survive. But with the advent of Norman rule, the posterity of this flourishing literature was postponed for almost a thousand years. *Beowulf*, probably composed in the eighth or ninth century, appeared in its first English edition in 1833. The undergraduate Alfred Tennyson had already turned a few lines of it into modern English verse. It was in Victoria's reign that the first poems in English became properly available to English readers and writers. Their reintroduction had a marked effect on the work of poets such as Henry Wadsworth Longfellow, William Morris and Gerard Hopkins, as well as Tennyson. And in the following century, to take only the best-known examples, the work of Ezra Pound, W. H. Auden and Geoffrey Hill clearly reflects the knowledge of Old English verse which they acquired at university.[2]

*   *   *

This book translates into verse a small selection of the earliest poems that remain. Before introducing the selection, one or two things need to be mentioned. First, the verse which Angles, Saxons, Jutes, Frisians, Franks and other Germanic settlers brought with them across the North Sea was composed, delivered and preserved without writing. (Speech precedes writing, which weakens the verbal memory on which oral composition relies.) The verse of all the Germanic peoples, from Austria to Iceland, had a common metrical basis. In Old English, this takes the form of a balance of stressed syllables in a set of five patterns with precise metrical requirements. These stressed syllables are not stressed in a way special to poetry but receive the vocal emphasis natural to spoken English. In this verse, the number of syllables is limited rather than fixed, and rhyme plays no part. The stressed syllables, receiving the stress they receive when spoken, are linked by the same initial sound. This is the origin of the term 'alliterative verse'. But alliteration, though more obvious, is a less fundamental characteristic of the metre than the stress-pattern which it indicates. The function of the alliteration is to act as a prompt to the composing poet, and to make the patterning of the stresses more salient to the ear of the hearer. Strictly speaking, alliteration applies to consonants, but the vowels represented in Old English by the letters, *a, e, i, o, u* and *y* are also deemed to alliterate with each other.

The chief rule of Old English verse-making is that one or other of the two syllables receiving the main stresses in the first half of the verse must alliterate with the first stressed syllable of the second half of the verse. The letter or sound beginning the third of these stressed syllables has to 'agree' with that beginning the first and/or the second stressed syllable. The fourth stress should not alliterate. Thus the first line of Tennyson's 'The Eagle' – 'He clasps the crag with crooked hands' – would be a regular line in Old English verse. Other regular lines, from my translations, are 'The fell and fen his fastness was' (said of Grendel), or (the first line of a riddle) 'I'm the world's wonder for I make women happy'.

It will be noticed that the line breaks into two halves, bound together by alliteration, and that the governing element is the first stress of the second half. An extended example from *Beowulf* follows, with the stressed syllables italicized and the mid-line pause marked by a space:

> Or a *fel*low of the *king's,*
> Whose *head* was a *store*house   of the *sto*ried *verse,*
> Whose *tongue gave   gold* to the *lan*guage
> Of the *trea*sured *re*pertory,   *wrought* a *new* lay
> *Made* in the *mea*sure.   The *man struck* up,
> *Found* the *phrase,   fram*ed *right*ly
> The *deed* of *Beow*ulf.

The five types of half-line could be further exemplified, but in an introduction to a book of translations this should suffice.

This metrical frame determines much in the style of Old English verse, which is largely cast in half-line units. The language was inflected: grammatical function is indicated by changes in the forms of words, usually in their terminations. Word order could be more variable than in modern English. In verse, the sense often seems to dance as it advances. A sentence of any length can unfold by taking two steps forward and one step back. Such a minuet-like movement of the sense is particularly noticeable in the style of *Beowulf*. This is in part a consequence of the formulaic component in the composition of verse. The poetry employs a traditional vocabulary, in which nouns are prominent and formulas for things commonly mentioned are multiplied and varied. The poetry of battle, for instance, will often refer to men, armour and weapons, and to death: to die is to fall among the dead, or among the fated, to choose rest or to choose God's light. The religious verse has a different vocabulary: the nine lines of *Cædmon's Hymn*, for example, include eight different names for God. Finding different ways of saying closely related things is a stylistic feature in Old English verse known as variation.

As well as a common metre and related poetic vocabularies, the verse of the Germanic peoples had a common fund of stories. A few of the Old English poems are set in an heroic age, which corresponds to the historical period when hosts of Goths, Vandals and their cousins overran the Roman Empire, a period known as the Wandering of the Peoples. The heroic poems set on the continent, such as *Widsith*, *Deor* and *The Fight at Finnsburgh*, have scarcely a trace of Christianity. *Beowulf* too is set in a heathen southern Scandinavia, but its story is told in a Christian light. The letters in which these poetic texts are preserved were formed by clerics. Indeed, some of the poetic riddles included in this book delight in pen and ink, and the steps involved in preparing and writing books, made of vellum. The English Church had no wish to preserve memories of the old heathen religion, and written references to heathenism are incidental and few.

The absence of pagan religion in the earliest literature in English disappointed nineteenth-century scholars and twentieth-century students hoping to find folk origins of a pre-Christian kind. These early northern philologists who often read vernacular texts in a spirit of Romantic nationalism had cut their teeth on classical rusks. They had read with interest the Roman historian Tacitus. In his *Germania* (AD 98), Tacitus has warlike Germanic armies preparing for battle by recalling the heroic deeds of their ancestors in song. These oral recitations were the only kind of literature they had, Tacitus tells us. His *Agricola* (a life of his father-in-law, a governor of Britannia), along with his *Annals*, are prime historical sources for the Roman conquest of Britain. They contain famous pages on the extermination of the Druids, and the revolt of Boudicca. Tacitus puts into the mouth of a British chieftain a speech to the troops which culminates in the epigram *solitudinem faciunt pacem appellant*: 'They make it a wilderness and call it peace' ('they' being the Romans). His liberty-loving Britons and heroic Germans express sophisticated 'republican' criticisms of the laxity and corruption of the Empire.

Some nineteenth-century scholars sympathetic to those anti-imperial or anti-Roman attitudes became confident that they could discriminate on stylistic grounds between the original parts of a text and the parts added by monastic scribes. Confidence in such analysis persisted through many editions of Henry Sweet's *Anglo-Saxon Reader*, first published in 1876 and still a set book for undergraduate students of English at the University of Oxford in 1980. In the present writer's copy of the fourteenth edition (1959), the text of *The Seafarer* ends at line 108. The remaining fifteen lines are relegated by the modern editor to the notes at the end of the book, with the comment: 'It is evident that the majority of these verses could not have formed part of the original poem.' The American poet Ezra Pound was therefore well within the limits of editorial orthodoxy when in 1914 he omitted from his famous version of *The Seafarer* what he called 'the pious but platitudinous address to the Deity' at its end. Pound went further, however. Wishing to return this Christian poem to its supposed heathen origins, he emended its text. Where the Old English gave 'angels', Pound chose to read 'Angles'. Bede has in his *History* a famous story in which Pope Gregory determines to turn the Angles into angels. Pound's *Seafarer* returns them to paganism, which was rather fashionable among intellectuals just before the outbreak of the First World War.[3]

Heroism is a major theme of Old English verse, and not only in the pan-Germanic poems set on the continent. The narrative tradition of oral composition celebrated not only courage and loyalty but also judgement and far-sightedness. Its role was to strengthen the morale and the insight of leaders in a society formed by war. But those who put the old oral tradition into writing were men of religion, and most of the extant verse is religious, often involving paraphrase of biblical stories. The treatment of these stories, however, is more heroic than modern English Christians are used to. Eleven of the twelve Apostles died as martyrs. *Andreas*, a verse life of St Andrew, begins:

> Listen! We have heard of twelve mighty heroes
> Honoured under heaven in days of old,
> Thanes of God. Their glory failed not
> In the clash of banners, the brunt of war,
> After they were scattered and spread abroad
> As their lots were cast by the Lord of heaven.
> Famous those heroes, foremost on earth,
> Brave-hearted leaders and bold in strife
> When hand and buckler defended the helm
> On the plain of war, on the field of fate.

> One was Matthew. . . .[4]

Some of the early English converts were inspired by the apostolic example of a missionary life and a martyr's death. Boniface of Crediton, a West Saxon who spent decades converting the continental Saxons and is known as the Apostle of the Germans, was hacked to death by heathens in Frisia in 754. In 641, the corpse of St Oswald, King of Northumbria, the victor of the Battle of Heavenfield but the loser of a subsequent battle, was mutilated and offered in sacrifice to the god Woden by the pagan king Penda of Mercia.

The old verse tradition had a mind-set which could more easily assimilate parts of the Old Testament, such as the deeds of Moses, of David or of Judith, than the Sermon on the Mount, loving one's enemies, or the theology of St Paul. The Old English verse paraphrases of the biblical books of Genesis, Exodus, Daniel and Judith emphasize the heroism of faith, as does *Andreas*. So does *Elene*, the story of St Helena's discovery of the True Cross, and so do two lives of St Guthlac, a seventh-century warrior prince victorious over demons in the Fens of East Anglia. There are also liturgical poems on Christ, a dramatic dialogue between Joseph and Mary, and a range of poems on moral, penitential and homiletic themes. Four of these poems are signed with the name 'Cynewulf'. Who Cynewulf was is unknown, perhaps a cleric of the ninth century.

The Christianity of these poems can be of a surprising kind, and many of them are narrative poems of a length to which modern readers have become unaccustomed. *Beowulf* is the only very substantial poem of the highest quality. If we leave it to one side, readers have admired the shorter poems, especially the so-called 'elegies' of the Exeter Book, such as *The Wanderer* and *The Seafarer*, and also *The Dream of the Rood*, an astonishing poem found in the Vercelli Book, an Old English manuscript of the late tenth century. *The Battle of Maldon* is a straightforward narrative of a battle against Danes in 991, a study in courage and loyalty. These four poems were regularly set for study at universities in 1960. Other short poems which equally repay reading include *The Ruin*, *Deor*, a set of narrative cameos with a repeated refrain, some Riddles in the Exeter Book and two dramatic love poems spoken by women, *Wulf and Eadwacer* and *The Wife's Lament*. The poems in this second list are shorter than those in the first set. They are also less obviously Christian, and more enigmatic.

Since the first of these translations was begun in 1959, scholarly knowledge has advanced, but the general readership in Britain for a book of this kind may be less well equipped than it used to be, in two respects. British schools used to teach an outline of national history, and formal English grammar, but in the 1970s discarded this kind of synoptic history and virtually abandoned the teaching of English grammar in any formal way. These decisions had unfortunate results. No longer taught at school, the period in which England was converted to Christianity and then united under a single monarchy slipped from national memory. As a result the world which made the poems translated here became more remote than it had been in 1959. The ditching of formal grammar made the precise appreciation of texts in unfamiliar languages far more difficult – although the poems in this volume are in translation, not in their original language. Yet access to older works of literature in the original becomes much more difficult without a proper knowledge of grammar, and the literature of the past thereby becomes more opaque to scrutiny and stylistic description. Other forms of access have improved since the 1960s, however, when the teaching of Anglo-Saxon history was dry and the teaching of Old English very dry. There was no attractive work of scholarly popularization such as James Campbell's *The Anglo-Saxons*, published in 1982. Yet the imaginative and literary quality of the poems translated here will appeal to any reader with curiosity and an open mind.

NOTES

1.   S. A. J. Bradley (ed. and tr.), *Anglo-Saxon Poetry* (London, 1982).
2.   Chris Jones, *Strange Likeness: The Use of Old English in Twentieth-century Poetry* (Oxford, 2006).
3.   See Michael Alexander, *The Poetic Achievement of Ezra Pound* (Edinburgh, 1998).
4.   C. W. Kennedy, *Early English Christian Poetry* (London, 1952), p. 122.

Further Reading

GENERAL

Bruce Mitchell and Fred C. Robinson, *A Guide to Old English*, 6th edn (Oxford, 2001), is a thorough introduction to the language, with sample passages and an annotated bibliography. Also recommended are: Stanley B. Greenfield and Daniel G. Calder, *A New Critical History of Old English Literature* (New York and London, 1986); Barbara C. Raw, *The Art and Background of Old English Poetry* (London, 1978); T. A. Shippey, *Old English Verse* (London, 1972); and C. L. Wrenn, *A Study of Old English Literature* (London, 1967). James Campbell (ed.), *The Anglo-Saxons* (Harmondsworth, 1991) is the best single introduction and handsomely illustrated. Michael Alexander, *A History of Old English Literature* (Peterborough, Ontario, 2002), provides a simple introduction. Indispensable for the early period is *Bede's Ecclesiastical History of the English People*, translated by L. Sherley-Price and by D. H. Farmer, rev. edn (Harmondsworth, 1990), or the World's Classics edition translated by Bernard Colgrave and edited by Judith McClure and Roger Collins (Oxford, 1999).

Allen, Michael J. B., and Calder, Daniel G., *Sources and Analogues of Old English Poetry: The Major Latin Texts in Translation* (Cambridge and Totowa, New Jersey, 1976).

Bjork, Robert E., and Niles, John D., *A Beowulf Handbook* (Lincoln, Nebraska, 1997).

Brown, Peter, *The Rise of Western Christendom*, 2nd edn (Oxford, 2003).

—, *The World of Late Antiquity* (London, 1971).

Bruce-Mitford, Rupert, *The Sutton Hoo Ship Burial*, 3 vols. (London, 1983).

Chadwick, H. M., and Chadwick, Nora K., *The Ancient Literature of Europe*, vol. 1 of *The Growth of Literature* (Cambridge, 1932).

Farmer, D. H., *The Oxford Dictionary of Saints*, 2nd edn (Oxford, 1987).

Finberg, H. P. R., *The Formation of England 550–1042* (London, 1974, 1976).

Ford, B. (ed.), *The Cambridge Guide to the Arts in Britain*, vol. 1 (Cambridge, 1988).

Henderson, George, *Early Medieval* (Harmondsworth, 1972).

Ker, W. P., *The Dark Ages* (London, 1904; Westport, Connecticut, 1979).

—, *Epic and Romance* (London, 1896; New York, 1957).

Lapidge, M., Blair, J., Keynes, S., and Scragg, D. (eds.), *The Blackwell's Encyclopaedia of Anglo-Saxon England* (Oxford, 1999).

Lapidge, M., and Godden, M., (eds.), *The Cambridge Companion to Old English Literature* (Cambridge, 1991).

Markus, R. A., *Gregory the Great and His World* (Cambridge, 1997).

Mayr-Harting, Henry, *The Coming of Christianity to Anglo-Saxon England* (London, 1972).

Nordenfalk, Carl, *Celtic and Anglo-Saxon Painting* (London, 1977).

Page, R. I., *Life in Anglo-Saxon England* (London, 1970).

Stenton, Sir Frank, *Anglo-Saxon England*, 3rd edn (Oxford, 1971).

Tacitus, Publius Cornelius, *Germania*, translated by H. S. Mattingly in *Tacitus on Britain and Germany* (Harmondsworth, 1950).

Whitelock, Dorothy, *The Audience of Beowulf*, 2nd edn (Oxford, 1958).

—, *The Beginnings of English Society* (Harmondsworth, 1960).

LANGUAGE

Davis, Norman, *Sweet's Anglo-Saxon Primer* (Oxford, 1953).
Quirk, Randolph, and Wrenn, C. L., *An Old English Grammar* (London, 1955).

EDITIONS

Alexander, Michael (ed.), *Beowulf: A Glossed Text*, Penguin English Poets, rev. edn (Harmondsworth, 2000).
—, and Riddy, F. J. (eds.), *The Macmillan Anthology of English Literature*, vol. 1: *The Middle Ages* (London, 1989).
Chambers, R. W. (ed.), *Widsith* (Cambridge, 1912).
Jack, George (ed.), *Beowulf: A Student Edition* (Oxford, 1994).
Krapp, G. P., and Dobbie, E. V. K., *The Anglo-Saxon Poetic Records*, 6 vols. (New York and London, 1931–54).
Muir, Bernard J. (ed.), *The Exeter Anthology of Old English Poetry*, 2 vols. (Exeter, 1994, 2000).
Pope, John C., *Seven Old English Poems*, 2nd edn (New York, 1981).
Scragg, D. G. (ed.), *The Battle of Maldon* (Manchester, 1981).
Swanton, M. (ed.), *The Dream of the Rood* (Manchester, 1970).
Treharne, Elaine (ed.), *Old and Middle English: An Anthology* (Oxford, 2000).
Whitelock, Dorothy, *Sweet's Anglo-Saxon Reader* (Oxford, 1970).

TRANSLATIONS

Alexander, Michael, *Beowulf: A Verse Translation*, 2nd edn (Harmondsworth, 2001).
—, *Old English Riddles from the Exeter Book*, rev. edn (London, 2007).
Bradley, S. A. J., *Anglo-Saxon Poetry* (London, 1982).

Garmonsway, G. N., *The Anglo-Saxon Chronicle* (London, 1953; New York, 1954).

—, and Simpson, J., *Beowulf and its Analogues* (London and New York, 1968).

Gordon, I. L., *The Seafarer*, Methuen's Old English Library (London, 1960).

Kershaw, N., *Anglo-Saxon and Norse Poems* (Cambridge, 1922).

Liuzza, R. M., *Beowulf: A New Verse Translation* (Peterborough, Ontario, 2000).

Swanton, Michael, *Anglo-Saxon Prose* (London and Totowa, New Jersey, 1975).

Whitelock, Dorothy, *English Historical Documents*, vol. 1: *500–1052*, 2nd edn (London, 1972).

— (ed.), with David C. Douglas and Susie I. Tucker, *The Anglo-Saxon Chronicle*, a revised translation (London, 1961).

A Note on the Translation

In 1966 I dedicated *The Earliest English Poems* to Ezra Pound, whose translation of *The Seafarer* I admired. I declared with equal boldness that I had never understood the point of translating poetry into prose; this was before I had read some of the verse translations of Old English poetry. Questions put to me since have made it clear that poetic translation (like Ezra Pound) is not generally understood. Hence this note.

Non-literary people have asked why translate something that has been translated before. Students of literature have asked why translations differ. A scholar even asked why a word was not translated by the same word each time it recurred. These questions presuppose that sense can be transposed directly from one language into another. This can suffice for asking the way to the railway station, but language can do more than convey information, and poetry does much more. Language would be simpler if a word meant only one thing, if the idea it denoted were universal, and if ideas could simply be downloaded into another language. Translation would then have no aim other than accuracy, and each word in a translation could automatically represent a word in the original. Translation would be as straightforward as brick-laying, with words instead of bricks. This kind of word-for-word glossing is accepted in examinations, yet language is far more complex than this rational and atomistic model assumes. The structures of languages differ, and the idiom of a language is governed by usage and custom as well as by rules, while the rules it obeys differ from the rules of logic.

Teaching English in provincial France in 1962, I was asked

by a senior colleague to name the poet who had written: '*Le beau, c'est affreux, et l'affreux, c'est beau.*' I did not know who it was, but when obliged to answer, I offered without conviction the name of Charles Baudelaire. '*Mais non! Shakespeere! Macbett!*' English ignorance of English literature was exposed. It may be that in French 'The horrible is the beautiful, and the beautiful is the horrible' is an equivalent of 'Fair is foul and foul is fair', but to an English ear this sounds too neat and abstract. Shakespeare's Rosaline says, towards the end of *Love's Labours Lost*,

> A jest's prosperity lies in the ear
> Of him that hears it, never in the tongue
> Of him that makes it.

This applies to more than jests. The above instance of languages at cross-purposes suggests, however, that each language has its own character, or rather that a language is engrained with the habitual assumptions of its users.

Language specialists would often prefer to confine translation to examination rooms, since for such scholars the primacy of the original text – or of its language – should not be challenged by translation. Translations can replace originals. It would suit language specialists for translation to remain secondary, dependent and servile, so that it could not be taken for the real thing.

If translation is not generally understood, the case of poetic translation is worse. Translation held a central place in English poetry until the nineteenth century. But when scientific philology arrived from Germany, accuracy became the supreme criterion in assessing translation. It was already a dominant criterion for the classical scholar Richard Bentley. When his opinion of Alexander Pope's translation of the *Iliad* was sought, Dr Bentley eventually had to say to the translator, 'A very pretty poem, Mr Pope, but you must not call it Homer.' Yet Dr Johnson, an excellent classicist, later judged Pope's *Iliad* 'a performance which no age or nation can pretend to equal'. Scholars since have tended to side with Bentley, but Johnson is the better critic.

Scholars can forget that translations are made for those who do not know the original. Those who know no Hebrew, Chinese or Russian may look at a translation to try to discover why the Psalms or Li Po or Pushkin are supposed to be of interest. They want to read something which reads well: faithful to the sense, certainly, but in an English which falls easily or interestingly on the ear, and whose manner suggests something of the style and even of the movement which recommend the original. Fidelity rather than accuracy is what is required. Accuracy is something, but the language a translator most needs to have at his command is his own language.

The study of languages must be kept up. Yet it remains a vital paradox that literature in dead languages can be living literature. Translators in love with their originals also believe that what is excellent can be made current. This conviction informed decisions taken when these translations were first undertaken. The first task of a verse translator is to decide on the appropriate form of verse. I decided to observe the metre of the original, including the alliteration, so far as I could do so in modern English without undue awkwardness. I wanted people to hear the old form of verse. This approximation involved endless patience. Each sentence was like a crossword. I calculate that each line of verse took about an hour, for the finished product had to read well. Few translators of Old English who aim at keeping the metre have tried hard to keep to the rules of that metre. Metrical regularity can only be achieved at some cost to natural idiom. Some scholars think the task impossible. One learned reviewer of my version of *Beowulf* described its policy of translation as choosing an especially gratuitous form of failure. I should add that in the making of the first translations, *The Ruin* and *The Wanderer*, metrical regularity was not the priority it became on the way to the final translations, those of *The Wife's Lament* and *The Seafarer*.

The next issue was idiom. What is the appropriate style for such translations? The diction of Old English poetry poses a special problem, for it is traditional, even archaic; many words used in verse are never found in prose. The archaic nature of Old English poetic diction aggravates the problem of translating from an earlier into a later form of the same language. An Italian translator of Virgil has a similar problem. Modern English has words which have changed little in form and usage: pronouns such as 'he', nouns such as 'man', 'sea' or 'day', verbs such as 'do', 'say' or 'hear'. Translation has no problem with such neutral words. Other words have disappeared: *leeds* has been replaced by 'people'. *Wyrd* is usually rendered by 'fate'. Words of French or Latin origin have different weights and connotations, but are often the best words. English was crossed with French after 1066, and to this mixture Latin was later added, followed by a sprinkling of Greek and other languages. The translations in this book favour words of English derivation – though only up to a point. Some old words have changed their meaning. *Dreary* no longer means 'blood-stained' and cannot be used in this sense. Others have become archaic: *byrnie* is a northern English word for a coat of mail, but it is risky to use it. The long craze for Walter Scott led, a century ago, to a suspicion of archaism, especially chivalric archaism. Too many swashes had been buckled, too many tushes tushed. Costume drama was henceforward for Hollywood.

It seemed nevertheless that the translation of Early English into Modern English was a business from which archaism could not with reason be ruled out. On occasion my versions risked 'atheling' (son of an *æthel* or nobleman), 'scop' (explained in the Introduction), 'wyrd' (spelled 'wierd' to differentiate it from 'weird') and 'linden' (limewood shield) – real Old English words, where modern alternatives were less good. One could take risks in a short poem. As I went on, the *-eth* form died the death. *Hwæt!* is the first word of several of the poems, a call for attention. A relic of oral performance, it can be translated as 'Listen' or 'Attend', but I have sometimes left it untranslated.

Please note that all line references are to the Old English texts.

This is the sense but not the order of the words as he sang them in his sleep; for verses, though never so well composed, cannot be literally translated out of one language into another without loss of their beauty and loftiness.

Bede, of Cædmon's Hymn

. . . tha ongan ic ongemang othrum mislicum and manigfealdum bisgum thisses kynerices tha boc wendan on Englisc . . . hwilum word be worde, hwilum andgit of angiete . . .

Alfred, of Gregory's Cura Pastoralis

THE RUIN

This description of a deserted Roman city is written on two leaves towards the back of the Exeter Book. A brand or a poker has been left to rest upon it, and there are holes in the vellum, or calf-skin, on which the words are written. The state of the text suggests the conditions in which manuscripts of Old English poetry survived, or did not survive. Monastic libraries were at risk from fires, usually accidental but sometimes deliberately started by Vikings. They later suffered at the hands of the agents of Thomas Cromwell. Unreadable old manuscripts could be put to various uses, including lighting the fire. The Exeter Book has been used as a cutting board and as a beer mat.

Massive building in stone is a Roman accomplishment which can still impress, and must have been all the more impressive to the Saxons, who built in wood and on a less grand scale. When the Romans pulled out of Britain after 410, they left many large stone buildings. Aquae Sulis, the Roman city of Bath, is the only city we know with a system fed by hot springs as described in this poem. The extensive ruins of Roman Bath stood in what became Wessex. The Saxons used stone only for churches, but such churches were small, like that of Aldhelm at Bradford on Avon, east of Bath. A large royal hall, such as that at Cheddar, south of Bath, was built of wood. The fourth word of the poem is *wealstan*, wallstone or masonry. *Weal* is one of the few English words borrowed from Latin: *vallum*, a rampart or wall. Roman roads left their mark on the British landscape and on the English language in the words 'street' and 'mile' and in place names such as the Fosse Way.

The *wealstan* is said to have been broken by Wierds, Fates,

and to have been built by giants. Other Old English poems also
speak of monumental buildings as having been constructed by
giants. The Saxons who saw these grand buildings had cause
for thought. The poet wonders at this fine city and at the skills
and the means of those who had built it and had abandoned
it. He imagines its builders and inhabitants as proud, a view
influenced by the Christian reaction to the Fall of Rome to the
Goths in 410. St Augustine of Hippo (354–430) expressed this
in his *City of God*, a heavenly city of love not an earthly city
of grandeur. The early Christians had regarded Rome as the
Israelites had regarded the empires of Egypt, Assyria and
Babylon. Christians were now in charge at Rome, but did not
regard it as an eternal city.

Gregory the Great (*c.*540–604), the architect of English
Christianity, had before becoming pope acted for six years as
Rome's ambassador to the city of Constantinople. The heir
to large Sicilian estates, which he sold to found monasteries,
Gregory knew that Rome's former greatness was much dimin-
ished, and how vulnerable it had become to barbarian attack.
Gregory's writings had authority in early Christian England.
He writes in his homily on Ezekiel: 'Where is now the Senate?
Where are the people? Where are they who rejoiced in the city's
glory? Where is their revelry?' The phrasing recalls the *SPQR*
proudly cut on monuments and public buildings throughout
the Empire: *Senatus populusque romanus*: ('The Senate and the
people of Rome'). This attitude to classical grandeur is found
in *The Wanderer* and *The Seafarer*, as well as in *The Ruin*.

The Ruin is like a number of poems in medieval Latin written
in praise of cities and on the fall of cities. But the particularity
with which it describes these buildings is not found elsewhere in
the surviving poetry, and its diction gives the poem an unusually
specific feel. The translation accordingly risks bold effects,
including archaisms. This was the first Old English poem I
translated, in 1959. The text is incomplete, and the translation
preserves its lacunae, the places where words are missing,
marked by ellipses.

The Ruin

Well-wrought this wall: Wierds broke it.
The stronghold burst. . . .

Snapped rooftrees, towers fallen,
the work of the Giants, the stonesmiths,
mouldereth.
                    Rime scoureth gatetowers
                    rime on mortar.

Shattered the showershields, roofs ruined,
age under-ate them.
                    And the wielders and wrights?
Earthgrip holds them – gone, long gone,
fast in gravesgrasp while fifty fathers
and sons have passed.
                    Wall stood,
grey lichen, red stone, kings fell often,
stood under storms, high arch crashed –
stands yet the wallstone, hacked by weapons,
by files grim-ground . . .
. . . shone the old skilled work
. . . sank to loam-crust.

Mood quickened mind, and a man of wit,
cunning in rings, bound bravely the wallbase
with iron, a wonder.

Bright were the buildings, halls where springs ran,
high, horngabled, much throng-noise;
these many mead-halls men filled
with loud cheerfulness: Wierd changed that.

Came days of pestilence, on all sides men fell dead,
death fetched off the flower of the people;
where they stood to fight, waste places
and on the acropolis, ruins.
                    Hosts who would build again

shrank to the earth. Therefore are these courts dreary
and that red arch twisteth tiles,
wryeth from roof-ridge, reacheth groundwards. . . .
Broken blocks. . . .
              There once many a man
mood-glad, goldbright, of gleams garnished,
flushed with wine-pride, flashing war-gear,
gazed on wrought gemstones, on gold, on silver,
on wealth held and hoarded, on light-filled amber,
on this bright burg of broad dominion.

Stood stone houses; wide streams welled
hot from source, and a wall all caught
in its bright bosom, that the baths were
hot at hall's hearth; that was fitting . . .
. . . .

Thence hot streams, loosed, ran over hoar stone
unto the ring-tank. . . .
    . . . It is a kingly thing
    . . . city. . . .

GNOMIC VERSES

The Gnomic Verses, also known as the Maxims, appear in the Exeter Book. They are collections of metrical proverbs. We still have rhyming saws such as 'Red sky at night, shepherd's delight' and family sayings such as 'A son is a son till he gets him a wife, but a daughter's a daughter all of her life'. It has been suggested that the collections may have been authorized by King Alfred. It is recorded of him by his biographer, Asser, Bishop of Sherborne, that he learned poems by heart as a child and that 'during the frequent wars and other difficulties . . . he continued to recite the Saxon books, and above all to learn the Saxon poems, and to make others learn them'. Certainly Alfred liked 'wisdom', a taste shared by many Anglo-Saxons, to judge by their literature. They especially liked the pithy or understated expression of wisdom. 'To avoid death is not easy' is a half-line in *Beowulf*, for instance. It is also not easy to express moral sententiousness without platitude, as can be seen even in Shakespeare. The poetry of the Gnomic Verses is very unlike most modern poetry.

The popular literature which remains includes charms against disease[1] and some physical riddles, but the Gnomic Verses have a special interest. The Australian poet A. D. Hope translated a few verses as follows:

> The dragon shall be in the mound,
> Wise, proud of his treasure; the fish in the water
> Bring forth its kind; the King shall in the hall
> Distribute rings; the bear shall be on the heath,
> Old and dreadful.[2]

The 'shall' found in each item in this list means both 'should' and 'always does'. 'Frost shall freeze / fire eat wood' is the first verse of the passage translated here. These are natural laws, like the quasi-scientific observations about the reproduction of fish and the habitat of bears, but such generalizations extend not only to kings and queens and sailors and sailors' wives, but also to dragons. Treasure buried under a mound suggests the barrows and megalithic tombs of the Stone Age, such as the one which is the lair of the dragon in *Beowulf*. Likewise the sixth-century funeral ship found at Sutton Hoo in Suffolk was buried under a mound by the seashore. The dragon in the mound may embody the curse attaching to those who disturb or re-use goods buried in a grave.

The generic habit of mind is fundamental in traditional societies, in which it is vital to understand and be prepared for the natural order inside which human beings live and die. The first lines of the following translation celebrate frost, fire, earth and ice, elements which directly affect physical life, though modern urban life insulates us against their effects. Here the world of pagan religion lies close to the surface. The wisdom literature of Old English poetry, like that of the Bible, celebrates the forces of the natural world, beautiful, impressive and frightening, and looks behind them to their creator. Here God is above all the Creator of the natural world: the 'One who all can'. It is He who, in the spring, 'free[s] the grain from wonder-lock'.

The translation is set out in such a way as to bring out the pattern of the half-lines of the original text.

Gnomic Verses
(lines 71–99)

Frost shall freeze
        fire eat wood
earth shall breed
        ice shall bridge
water a shield wear.
        One shall break
frost's fetters
        free the grain
from wonder-lock
        – One who all can.

Winter shall wane
        fair weather come again
the sun-warmed summer!
        The sound unstill
the deep dead wave
        is darkest longest.
Holly shall to the pyre
        hoard be scattered
when the body's numb.
        Name is best.

A king shall win
        a queen with goods
beakers, bracelets.
        Both must first
be kind with gifts.
        Courage must wax
war-mood in the man,
        the woman grow up
beloved among her people,
        be light of mood
hold close a rune-word
        be roomy-hearted
at hoard-share and horse-giving.

When the hall drinks
she shall always and everywhere
                    before any company
greet first
                    the father of athelings
with the first draught
                    – deft to his hand she
holds the horn –
                    and when they are at home
                                        together
know the right way
                    to run their household.

The ship must be nailed
                    the shield framed
from the light linden.
                    But how loving the welcome
of the Frisian wife
                    when floats offshore
the keel come home again!
                    She calls him within walls,
her own husband
                    – hull's at anchor! –
washes salt-stains
                    from his stiff shirt
brings out clothes
                    clean and fresh
for her lord on land again.
                    Love's need is met.

THE EXETER RIDDLES

I heard of a wonder, of words moth-eaten;
that is a strange thing, I thought, weird
that man's song be swallowed by a worm,
his binded sentences, his bedside stand-by,
rustled in the night – and the robber-guest
not one whit the wiser for the words he had mumbled.

The Exeter Book is a manuscript left to Exeter Cathedral in
1072 by its bishop, Leofric. It is a collection of poems, among
them ninety-four riddles, and when the manuscript was com-
plete there may have been a hundred riddles. The pages of the
book are of calf-skin, vellum. The man who traced out the first
words of the Old English riddle, *Moððe word fræt*, translated
above, knew that the bookworm moth likes calf-skin, and that
the wisdom preserved in verse and stored in his writing might
be inwardly digested by a moth.

The scribe who wrote the book in about 970, though aware
of its vulnerability to bookworm and to fire, may not have
considered the possibility that his language itself might perish.
Yet by the time of the death of the bishop who left the book in
his will, English was not the language of the rulers of the land,
who referred to it as Angleterre or even as Outre-Manche. By
1100, English was being written only in monasteries. It came
back to the surface eventually, in a much altered state. An
understanding of the older form of the language was recovered
very much later, by the accumulated efforts of generations of
scholars. It was reasonably understood by 1830, when the
undergraduate Tennyson translated a few lines from *Beowulf*

into a notebook: 'The enemy's leader / His wordhoard unlocked...' His college friend J. M. Kemble produced the first English edition of *Beowulf* in 1833. Tennyson's 'The Eagle' is a riddle, and, as has been noted in the Introduction, its first line – 'He clasps the crag with crooked hands' – observes Old English alliteration. Some of the Exeter Riddles are as good poetically as 'The Eagle', but they lack the heroic gloom popularly expected of Old English verse. The Riddles receive a very much fuller introduction here than is usual, because they isolate a verbal indirectness – a guess-inviting quality – which is basic to the old vernacular poetry in general. The Riddles deserve to be enjoyed more widely. It is good that they are increasingly included in the first poems now studied.

The Exeter Book gives no authors and no titles to the 193 poems it now contains; nor are solutions given for the Riddles. Most are more elusive than 'Bookworm'. Riddle 75 consists of a single line of verse: *Ic ane geseah idese sittan*. Literally construed, this reads: 'I a single saw woman sitting'; the adjective *ane* (one) qualifies the noun *idese* (woman). My first translation of this read: 'I saw a woman sit alone'. Initial vowels alliterate in Old English verse; *ane* and *idese* agree in sound as well as grammatically; both are in the accusative case.

Some scholars have thought this one-line riddle incomplete. It had no accepted solution. A woman might sit alone for various reasons. I received a postcard which suggested that the answer might be 'A Hen'. Another reader wrote proposing 'The Moon', which was attractive, though Old English *se mona* is masculine. I remained undecided, assuming all the while that the woman must be the subject. She might be lonely, like the women who speak the Exeter Book poems *Wulf and Eadwacer* and *The Wife's Lament*; or like the speaker of Ezra Pound's version translated from the Chinese, 'The Jewel Stair's Grievance'. I was still looking in this direction when another postcard came with what must be the correct solution: 'A Mirror'.

Exeter Riddles are either 'I Am' riddles (a non-human creature or thing is given speech) or 'I Saw' riddles (a creature/thing is described). The 'I Am' type is more common, and the Mirror is an 'I Am' riddle camouflaged as an 'I Saw' riddle. The 'I' of

Ic geseah is not a human speaker. Old English *ides* (nominative form) properly means not 'woman' but 'lady', and a polished metal mirror might belong to a lady rather than a woman. The translation changed into 'I saw a lady sitting alone'. This story shows that a translator needs to know the solution to a riddle before he begins to translate it. (I say 'he' because although there are many women among scholars of Old English, women have not, so far as I know, translated the Riddles.)

Some riddles, like those on the Swan and the Cuckoo (Riddles 7 and 9), are clear enough. The Ice riddle (number 68) ends 'Water became bone'. The subjects are either natural or things about the house. A riddle can be a simple paradox: the bookworm devours books but learns nothing. Some have a deeper wit.

> My home is not silent: I myself am not loud.
> The Lord has provided for the pair of us
> a joint expedition. I am speedier than he
> and sometimes stronger; he stays the course better.
> Sometimes I rest, but he runs on.
> For as long as I live, I live in him;
> if we leave one another, it is I who must die.

This is a version of the Latin '*Flumen et piscis*' by Symphosius, a writer of the fourth or fifth century AD who left a hundred three-line riddles. Symphosius' riddles have titles. One translator of the Exeter version also provided the title 'Fish and River'.

The Italian proverb '*traditore traddutore*' says that translators betray what they translate. Since languages and cultures differ, most of the elusive qualities evaporate in the translation of a poem, and what replaces them is often inappropriate. But to advertise a riddle's solution in advance spoils the game. Although I have given some solutions and proposed others in introducing the Riddles, the best place for solutions is at the back of a book.

A riddle's answer should not be too obvious. Obliquity was enjoyed by the Anglo-Saxons. They do not assume that the meaning of life's events is simple; they turn things over in their

verse, usually slowly. When something is well known, they find
ways of presenting it under another aspect. One such way is
severe understatement, as in *Beowulf*'s half-line 'To avoid death
is not easy'. Seamus Heaney describes the style of *Beowulf*
as 'direct' and 'constantly in the indicative mood'. These are
qualities he gives his translation, but I would have to disagree
with this characterization of the original. The style of *Beowulf*
can be bold, yet its many reflective passages are in the subjunc-
tive mood, and its style and narrative method are often indirect
– as indicated in the half-line quoted above. Unstraightfor-
wardness is common in Old English poetry as a whole, not only
in the Riddles.

In Charles Dickens's *Our Mutual Friend*, Mr Podsnap has
a daughter. Famously, for Mr Podsnap, 'The question about
everything was, would it bring a blush into the cheek of the
young person.' Some of the Exeter Riddles might bring a
wrinkle to the brow of a teacher. Broaching this topic, A. J.
Wyatt, in his edition of a century ago, remarked upon 'the
absence of lubricity' in Old English verse, a phrase showing an
elegant indirection no longer characteristic of academic editors.
The few riddles which are indecent have innocent solutions,
and their translator has to keep the reader's options open.
'Swings by his thigh a thing most magical' is the first line of the
Key. Here is another riddle (number 25) from which lubricity
is technically absent:

> I'm the world's wonder, for I make women happy
> – a boon to the neighbourhood, a bane to no one,
> though I may pain a little the one who picks me.
>
> I am set well up, stand in a bed,
> have a roughish root. Rarely (though it happens)
> a churl's daughter more daring than the rest
> – and lovelier! – lays hold of me,
> rushes my red top, wrenches at my head,
> and lays me in the larder.
>   She learns soon enough,
> the curly-haired creature who clamps me so,
> of my meeting with her: moist is her eye!

The Anglo-Saxons liked heroic poetry, but they could enjoy the wit of a riddle about an onion. They began as conquerors, but they turned their swords into ploughshares, and most of them became farmers. For the warrior class among them, there were many winter evenings to pass between the arrival of Hengest in 449 and the death of Harold in 1066. Poetry was a help, riddles were a help. The composition of Old English verse, like the ruminative enjoyment of riddles, preceded literacy, brought to the English by the Roman mission in 597.

Alfred of Wessex (d. 899) was illiterate until he was twelve, though his Welsh biographer tells us that he already loved listening to poetry and reciting it. A successful general, Alfred saved Wessex from the Danes, and persuaded their leader to adopt Christianity and to go away. His kingdom safe, Alfred learned to read Latin. He encouraged vernacular learning, as stated previously, learned to write himself, commissioned translations and wrote valuable books. Old English verse is Christian in that the only clerks were clerics, but the poems are of various kinds. Bishop Leofric's book includes religious poems, philosophical elegies such as *The Ruin* and *The Wanderer*, and poems about the love of women for men, and vice versa. Its riddles are of various kinds also.

Riddles are as ancient as the riddle of the Sphinx, solved by Oedipus: 'What animal goes on four legs in the morning, on two at noon, and on three in the evening?' (Man). In the Book of Judges, Samson put a riddle to the Philistines: 'Out of the eater came forth meat, and out of the strong came forth sweetness.'[1] He had found bees, and honey, in the carcass of a lion he had killed. Hence the image on the Tate & Lyle syrup tin.

Riddles are traditional, popular, literary and mixed. There was a craze in the Catholic hierarchy of England for writing Latin riddles, which reached its peak about the year 700. St Aldhelm, Bishop of Sherborne, wrote clever *Aenigmata* (the Greek word for riddles). Other riddle writers were an Archbishop of Canterbury, an Abbot of Wearmouth and two more saints: Boniface, the Apostle of the Germans, and Bede. These clergymen were not beef-witted biffers of Celts, but more like the Foreign Office mandarins of legend who, after solving a border dispute, composed Latin verse in the bath and did *The Times* crossword using the Across clues only.

It was a former member of the Foreign Office who solved one of the unsolved Old English riddles. The translation of Riddle 73 used to read:

> I was a pure girl and a grey-maned woman,
> a fair-faced man, a fresh girl,
> floated on foam, flew with birds,
> under the wave dived, dead among fish,
> and walked upon land a living soul.

The note in *Old English Riddles from the Exeter Book* (the larger selection of riddles commissioned by Anvil Press) explained that the proposed solution, 'A Mermaid', accorded with what seems to have been believed about mermaids. The book was reviewed by Arthur Cooper, author of the Penguin Classic *Li Po and Tu Fu*. Cooper collected languages, and was a scholar of Chinese and Japanese. The European languages he knew included Old Irish and Old Icelandic but not Old English. He read my translation, and, dissatisfied by my version, asked me to check the grammatical gender of the Old English word for snow. I reported that it was masculine. He asked what 'fair-faced man' stood for in the original. I told him that it was *ænlic rinc*. Recognizing *rinc* from Icelandic, Cooper asked if *ænlic* could mean 'unique'. It could. The answer must be 'Snow', he said, as in Icelandic poetry the crest of a hill covered in snow is likened to the mane of a grey horse. Arthur Cooper, a former cryptographer in British Intelligence and accustomed to mind-bending, said that *ænlic rinc* was a clue that the answer to the riddle must be a masculine singular noun. His 'Snow' changed my translation of the line and of the riddle as a whole.

The clerical riddlers of AD 700 were the Intelligence of the clerical hierarchy. St Aldhelm of Sherborne paraded his Latin learning. He wrote a prose treatise on virginity for a convent of nuns at Barking, and then rewrote it in verse. The epistle on metrics which he addressed to a King of Northumbria is full of riddles he had composed to exemplify different metres. His verbal gymnastics can be painful.

But why did these religious men set themselves to writing metrical and linguistic exercises? Why did the brain beneath the tonsure need to be teased? Because exercise with words improved the understanding of the Scriptures, read each day by monks and nuns. Words were needed to construe the Word. Bede wrote twenty-five works of biblical commentary before relaxing with his history of the English Church and people. Besides their Latin poems, Bede and Aldhelm are described as improvising Old English verses in public. It was unusual for such oral performance of vernacular verse to be thought worth preserving in written form.

These serious men wrote riddles on natural things – birds, ice, storms – and on things which sustained human life: barley, dough, honey, oxen, poultry, fish, oysters, horn, wood, metal, weapons, books. There are several about books, such as Riddle 51:

> I saw four fine creatures
> travelling in company; their tracks were dark,
> their trail very black. The bird that floats
> in the air swoops less swiftly than their leader;
> he dived beneath the wave. Drudgery was it
> for the fellow that taught all four of them their ways
> on their repeated visits to the vessel of gold.

The 'leader' is the index finger which drives the quill; the 'drudge' is the scribe himself; the solution, 'A Hand Writing'. Another riddle, number 26, begins 'I am the scalp of myself, skinned by my foeman'. The speaker is a codex made of calf-skin, which describes the preparation of vellum, its cutting, and the hand writing upon it, then the jewelsmith's binding. It is the most precious and useful of books: a Gospel Book.

Riddles use wit and words on nature and on man's use of nature. Their focus is often domestic, unlike that of most Old English verse. It is useful, however, to encounter some riddles

before reading too many other poems, and to remember that
Anglo-Saxon society was based on farming, even if its surviving
verse is mostly either aristocratic or spiritual or both. The
nature riddles can be exalted, even so. The first three Exeter
Riddles are about storms, and resemble the wisdom literature
of the Old Testament. One riddle-poem not in the Exeter Book
needs to be mentioned in conclusion. *The Dream of the Rood*
is a dream-vision, in which the Cross of the Crucifixion itself
speaks to the Dreamer. It follows immediately after the Riddles
in this book.

The speech of the Rood or Cross, which forms the core of
The Dream of the Rood, was carved on a stone cross early in
the eighth century. This stone text is among the earliest Old
English verse. The Exeter Riddles are, among other things, a
good preparation for reading it. Riddle 30 is especially apposite.

> I am fire-fretted and I flirt with Wind
> and my limbs are light-freighted and I am lapped in flame
> and I am storm-stacked and I strain to fly
> and I am a grove leaf-bearing and a glowing ember.
>
> From hand to friend's hand about the hall I go,
> so much do lords and ladies love to kiss me.
> When I hold myself high, and the whole company
> bow quiet before me, their blessedness
> shall flourish skyward beneath my fostering shade.

The solution is Wood, in various forms; the final two a cup and
a cross. The Cross which speaks to the Dreamer in the greater
poem is, like Wood, several things at once. One moment it is
stained with the blood of the Crucifixion, the next glorious
with the gold of the Resurrection. This Christian paradox found
ideal expression in a form dear to the newly converted Anglo-
Saxons – the riddle.

Please see Proposed Solutions to the Riddles, at the end of
this book, for suggested solutions to the riddles presented here.

7

When it is earth I tread, make tracks upon water
or keep the houses, hushed is my clothing,
clothing that can hoist me above house-ridges,
at times toss me into the tall heaven
where the strong cloud-wind carries me on
over cities and countries; accoutrements that
throb out sound, thrilling strokes
deep-soughing song, as I sail alone
over field and flood, faring on,
resting nowhere. My name is * * * *.

9

Abandoned unborn by my begetters
I was still dead a few spring days ago:
no beat in the breast, no breath in me.

A kinswoman covered me in the clothes she wore,
no kind but kind indeed. I was coddled and swaddled
as close as I had been a baby of her own,
until, as had been shaped, so shielded, though no kin,
the unguessed guest grew great with life.

She fended for me, fostered me, she fed me up,
till I was of a size to set my bounds
further afield. She had fewer dear
sons and daughters because she did so.

12

While my ghost lives I go on feet,
rend the ground, green leas.

When breath is gone I bind the hands
of swart Welsh; worthier men, too.

I may be a bottle: bold warrior
swigs from my belly.
                                    Or a bride may set
proudly her foot on me.
                                    Or, far from her Wales,
a dark-headed girl grabs and squeezes me,
silly with drink, and in the dark night
wets me with water, or warms me up
before the fire. Fetched between breasts
by her hot hand, while she heaves about
I must stroke her swart part.
                                    Say my name:
who living live off the land's wealth
and, when dead, drudge for men.

25

I'm the world's wonder, for I make women happy
– a boon to the neighbourhood, a bane to no one,
though I may pain a little the one who picks me.

I am set well up, stand in a bed,
have a roughish root. Rarely (though it happens)
a churl's daughter more daring than the rest
– and lovelier! – lays hold of me,
rushes my red top, wrenches at my head,
and lays me in the larder.
                                    She learns soon enough,
the curly-haired creature who clamps me so,
of my meeting with her: moist is her eye!

26

I am the scalp of myself, skinned by my foeman:
robbed of my strength, he steeped and soaked me,
dipped me in water, whipped me out again,
set me in the sun. I soon lost there
the hairs I had had.
                          The hard edge
of a keen-ground knife cuts me now,
fingers fold me, and a fowl's pride
drives its treasure trail across me;
bounds again over the brown rim,
sucks the wood-dye, steps again on me,
makes his black marks.
                          A man then hides me
between stout shield-boards stretched with hide,
fits me with gold. There glows on me
the jewelsmith's handiwork held with wires.

Let these royal enrichments and this red dye
and splendid settings spread the glory
of the Protector of the peoples – and not plague the fool.
If the sons of men will make use of me
they shall be the safer and the surer of victory,
the wiser in soul, the sounder in heart,
the happier in mind. They shall have the more friends,
loving and kinsmanlike, kind and loyal,
good ones and true, who will gladly increase
their honour and happiness, and, heaping upon them
graces and blessings, in the embraces of love
will clasp them firmly. Find out how I am called,
my celebrated name, who in myself am holy,
am of such service, and salutary to men.

27

Men are fond of me. I am found everywhere,
brought in from the woods and the beetling cliffs,
from down and from dale. In the daylight wings
raised me aloft, then into a roof's shade
swung me in sweetly. Sweltered then
by men in a bath, I am a binder now,
soon a thrasher, a thrower next:
I'll put an old fellow flat on the ground.
A man who tries to take me on,
tests my strength, soon finds out,
if his silly plan doesn't pall on him,
that it is his back that will hit the dust.
Loud in words, he has lost control
of his hands and feet, and his head doesn't work:
his strength has gone. Guess my name
who have such mastery of men on earth
that I knock them about in broad daylight.

29

A curious and wonderful creature I saw
– bright air-grail, brave artefact –
homing from a raid with its haul of silver
brimming precarious crescent horns.

To build itself a hideaway high up in the city,
a room in a tower, timbered with art,
was all it aimed at, if only it might.

Then over the wall rose a wonder familiar
to the earth-race, to everyone known.
It gathered to itself the hoard, and to its home drove off
that unhappy outcast. Onward it coursed,
wandered westward with wasting heart.

Dust rose to the skies, dew fell to the earth,
night was no more. No man knew
along what ways it wandered after.

30

I am fire-fretted and I flirt with Wind
and my limbs are light-freighted and I am lapped in
        flame
and I am storm-stacked and I strain to fly
and I am a grove leaf-bearing and a glowing ember.

From hand to friend's hand about the hall I go,
so much do lords and ladies love to kiss me.
When I hold myself high, and the whole company
bow quiet before me, their blessedness
shall flourish skyward beneath my fostering shade.

33

Strange the creature that stole through the water.
Grandly she called from her keel to the land,
lifted her loud voice. Her laughter was fearful,
awful where it was known; her edges sharp.
Slow to enter, she was not slack in battle;
hard, and, in deeds of destruction, unyielding:
she crushed wooden walls. Wicked the spell
that she cunningly unbound about her creation:
'My mother – and I am the most daring
of all the sex – is also my daughter
when grown up in strength. It is granted likewise
by the wise among the people, that in every part of the
        earth,
in whatever station, she stands gracefully.'

34

She feeds the cattle, this creature I have seen
in the houses of men. Many are her teeth
and her nose is of service to her. Netherward she goes,
loyally plundering and pulling home again;
she hunts about the walls in hope of plants,
finding always some that are not firmly set.
She leaves the fair fast-rooted ones
to stand undisturbed in their established place,
brightly shining, blossoming and growing.

35

The womb of the wold, wet and cold,
bore me at first, brought me forth.
I know in my mind my making was not
through skill with fells or fleeces of wool;
there was no winding of wefts, there is no woof in me,
no thread thrumming under the thrash of strokes,
no whirring shuttle steered through me,
no weaver's reed rapped my sides.
The worms that braid the broidered silk
with Wierd cunning did not weave me;
yet anywhere over the earth's breadth
men will attest me a trustworthy garment.

Say truly, supple-minded man,
wise in words, what my name is.

38

I watched a beast of the weaponed sex.
He forced, fired by the first of lusts,
four fountains which refreshed his youth
to shoot out shining in their shaped ways.

A man stood by that said to me:
'That beast, living, will break clods;
torn to tatters, will tie men's hands.'

42

I saw two wonderful and weird creatures
out in the open unashamedly
fall a-coupling. If the fit worked,
the proud blonde in her furbelows got
what fills women.
                    The floor's my table:
the runes I trace tell any man
acquainted with books both the creatures'
names in one.
                    Need (N) shall be there
twice over; two Oaks (A);
and the bright Ash (Æ) – one only in the line –
and Hail (H) twice too.
                    Who the hoard's door
with a key's power can unlock
that guards the riddle against rune-guessers,
holds its heart close, hides it loyally
with cunning bonds?
                    Clear now
to men at wine by what names
this shameless couple are called among us.

43

I know of one who is noble and brave,
a guest in our courts. Neither grim hunger
nor hot thirst can harm him at all,
neither age nor illness. If only the servant
whom on his journey he has to have with him
serves him faithfully, they shall find appointed,
when safe in their homeland, happiness and feasting,
untold bliss – but bitterness otherwise,
if the lord's servant serves his master
ill on the way. One must not be
a burden to his brother or both will suffer
when they are jointly drawn on their journey
    elsewhere
and must leave the company of the kinswoman
    who is
their only sister and their mother. Let the man
    who will,
declare graciously how the guest might be called,
or else the servant, whom I speak of here.

44

Swings by his thigh a thing most magical!
Below the belt, beneath the folds
of his clothes it hangs, a hole in its front end,
stiff-set and stout, but swivels about.

Levelling the head of this hanging instrument,
its wielder hoists his hem above the knee:
it is his will to fill a well-known hole
that it fits fully when at full length.

He has often filled it before. Now he fills it again.

47

I heard of a wonder, of words moth-eaten;
that is a strange thing, I thought, weird
that a man's song be swallowed by a worm,
his binded sentences, his bedside stand-by
rustled in the night – and the robber-guest
not one whit the wiser for the words he had
     mumbled.

50

There is on earth a warrior wonderfully engendered:
between two dumb creatures it is drawn into
     brightness
for the use of men. Meaning harm, a foe
bears it against his foe. Fierce in its strength,
a woman may tame it. Well will he heed
and meekly serve both men and women
if they have the trick of tending him,
and feed him properly. He promotes their happiness,
enhances their lives. Allowed to become
proud, however, he proves ungrateful.

51

I saw four fine creatures
travelling in company; their tracks were dark,
their trail very black. The bird that floats
in the air swoops less swiftly than their leader;
he dived beneath the wave. Drudgery was it
for the fellow that taught all four of them their ways
on their repeated visits to the vessel of gold.

57

Their dark bodies, dun-coated,
when the breeze bears them up over the backs of
   the hills
are black, diminutive.
                 Bold singers,
they go in companies, call out loudly;
they tread the timbered cliff, and at times the eaves
of men's houses.
                 How do they call themselves?

60

I was by the sand at the sea-wall once:
where the tide comes I kept my dwelling,
fast in my first seat. There were few indeed
of human kind who cared to behold
my homeland in that lonely place,
but in every dawning the dark wave
lapped about me. Little did I think
that early or late I ever should
speak across the meadbench, mouthless as I am,
compose a message. It is a mysterious thing,
dark to the mind that does not know,
how a knife's point and a clever hand,
a man's purpose and a point also,
have pressed upon me to the purpose that
I might fearlessly announce, for none but us two,
a message to you, so that no man beside
might spread abroad what is spoken between us.

68

The wave, over the wave, a wierd thing I saw,
thorough-wrought, and wonderfully ornate:
a wonder on the wave – water become bone.

69

The thing is magic, unimaginable
to him who knows not how it is.
It throstles through its sides, its throat angled
and turned with knowledge, two barrels
set sharp on the shoulder.
                              Its shaping is fulfilled
as it stands by the wayside so wonderful to see,
tall and gleaming, to glad the passer-by.

73

I was a pure girl and a grey-maned woman
and, at the same time, a singular man.
I flew with the birds, breasted the sea,
sank beneath the wave, dissolved among fish
and alighted on land. I had a living soul.

75

I saw a lady sitting alone.

76

I fed in the deep folds of the sea:
waves covered me, close to the land.
Often to the ocean I opened my mouth:
foot had I none. Now my flesh will be
meat for a man. He'll not mind my outside
once his knife's sharpness has sheared a way
between me and my hide. Hastily then
he'll eat me, uncooked . . .

79

Hwæt!
        I am always at the atheling's shoulder,
his battle-fellow, bound to him in love.
I follow the king. Flaxen-headed
lady may lay her light hand on me,
though she be of clearest blood, an earl's child.
I hold in my heart the hollow tree's fruit,
ride out in front on a fierce steed
when the host goes harrying, harsh-tongued then,
bear to songsmith when singing's done
his word-won gift. I have a good nature,
and in myself am swart. Say what I am called.

80

I am puff-breasted, proud-crested,
a head I have, and a high tail,
eyes and ears and one foot,
both my sides, a back that's hollow,

a very stout beak, a steeple neck
and a home above men.
                              Harsh are my sufferings
when that which makes the forest tremble takes and
    shakes me.
Here I stand under streaming rain
and blinding sleet, stoned by hail;
freezes the frost and falls the snow
on me stuck-bellied. And I stick it all out
for I cannot change the chance that made me.

84

My home is not silent: I myself am not loud.
The Lord has provided for the pair of us
a joint expedition. I am speedier than he
and sometimes stronger; he stays the course better.
Sometimes I rest, but he runs on.
For as long as I live, I live in him;
if we leave one another, it is I who must die.

85

Many were met, men of discretion,
wisdom and wit, when in there walked. . . .

Two ears it had, and one eye solo,
two feet and twelve hundred heads,
back, belly, a brace of hands,
a pair of sides and shoulders and arms
and one neck. Name, please.

THE DREAM OF
THE ROOD

The Dream of the Rood is a poem of 156 lines. It recounts the Dreamer's vision of the cross on which Christ was crucified. In this dream the Cross speaks to him and tells him of its part in the Crucifixion; then of how it was afterwards buried but eventually recovered. A rood is a cross, notably the kind of cross that stood on the rood screens which divided the nave from the sanctuary in a medieval church: a tall cross bearing the crucified Christ, with his mother and St John looking up at him from either side. 'Rood' is now distinctly archaic and 'A Vision of the Cross' would make a less mysterious title, if the old title were not already established. The text of the poem is found in the Vercelli Book, a manuscript in the library of the cathedral of St Andrew at Vercelli, an Italian city at the foot of the Alps on the road to Rome; a road taken by Anglo-Saxons going on foot *ad limina apostolorum*, to the precincts of the Apostles, where Peter and Paul were martyred. These Saxon pilgrims were numerous, and Rome had a Saxon quarter as a result. Several Saxon kings retired to die near the tombs of the martyrs. The Vercelli manuscript, written in Late West Saxon, also contains two long poems, *Andreas*, a life of St Andrew, and *Elene*, a life of St Helena, and some homilies in prose. The manuscript is dated to the late tenth century.

Fifteen lines of the same text, in Northumbrian dialect, are to be found carved on a much earlier artefact – a tall sandstone cross at Ruthwell, in Dumfries, Scotland, not far from Carlisle and the west end of the border with England. Ruthwell is pronounced Ruth'll or Rivell. This standing cross is 5.28 metres in height. Its front, back and sides are covered with a set of panels depicting sacred scenes in deep relief. The theological programme of these scenes comes from the Mediterranean, and the sculptural figures are Roman in style. (The many Celtic high crosses of this period are different in style and normally lack human figures.) The sculptural panels are surrounded by inscriptions, mostly in runic letters, which have nothing in common with the letter-forms of modern alphabets. Runes are an early Germanic script which could be used for cryptic purposes. The runes at Ruthwell were deciphered in 1840 by the scholar and historian J. M. Kemble.

The panels have titles in Latin, but the inscription running round the cross is in Northumbrian English, and in runic characters. Like the Lindisfarne Gospels and the work of Bede, the Ruthwell Cross is a monument of the Golden Age of Northumbria. The cross is of the early eighth century, so Bede (c. 672–735) may well have known the poem's author. After standing in the open air for nearly a thousand years, the cross was in 1642 broken into pieces by order of the General Assembly of the Church of Scotland as an idolatrous monument. In 1802 it was reassembled and re-erected by the parish minister, and placed inside the church. The runic inscription in English is damaged but ran to about fifty lines. It was part of the Rood's original design, and is one of the earliest surviving poetic texts. The title *The Dream of the Rood*, however, is properly reserved to the expanded text which appeared in the Vercelli Book two and a half centuries later.

Finally, two lines quoted from the poem are incised on a silver reliquary of the early eleventh century at the church of SS Michel-et-Gudule in Brussels. Inside is a fragment of the True Cross. The quotation runs:

> + *rod is min nama; geo ic ricne Cyning bær bifigynde,*
>   *blode bestemed*

> Rood is my name; once, trembling, covered with blood,
>   I bore the great King

In the Middle Ages, the exact form of a text was reproduced
only in the case of sacred texts; vernacular texts normally vary.
This Old English poem on the Cross exists in three forms,
traced on stone, and on calf-skin, and on silver, though this last
is a quotation, not a full text. None is in England now, although
the Ruthwell Cross was part of an English mission into what is
now Scotland.

'Rood is my name': the cult of the Cross of the Crucifixion
was widespread in the late Roman Empire and early Christian
Europe. Christians believed that in the reign of the Emperor
Constantine, early in the fourth century, the cross on which
Christ had been crucified had been discovered and taken to
Rome. The discovery of the True Cross was later in that century
associated with St Helena. By then Christianity was the official
religion of the Roman Empire, a change which had begun
with the conversion of Constantine. Constantine, the son of an
emperor, attributed his becoming emperor to a vision of the
cross: a heavenly vision granted to him on the eve of his victory
over his rival at the Battle of the Milvian Bridge, north of Rome,
in 312. In his dream he was told *in hoc signum vincis*: 'It is in
this sign that you conquer'. A crucial vision indeed. In 313
Constantine proclaimed Toleration for Christianity through-
out an empire which, a few years earlier, under the emperors
Diocletian and Galerius, had put many Christians to death.
Constantine moved slowly to becoming Christian himself. He
built the Basilica of the Holy Sepulchre in Jerusalem, and other
shrines in the Holy Land. The sign of the cross quietly used
by Christians before Toleration was now placed on Christian
churches, and became part of the insignia of the Empire of
Rome and of its new eastern capital at Constantinople. Yet
Constantine had been born in York, and it was from York that
he had begun his march on Rome. His mother was Helena,
wife of Constantius Clorus, a general who later became
emperor. Helena became a Christian in 312, when she was over
sixty, and went to the Holy Land in search of the cross on
which Christ suffered, as is recounted in the poem *Elene*, also
in the Vercelli Book. In some versions of Helena's legend, she
is a British princess.

The genuineness of the True Cross seems unlikely, and the physicality of its cult seems exceedingly strange today. Yet what is strange can be understood by the patient enquirer. Such forms of worship grew out of the meetings at which the first Christians commemorated Christ and his Apostles, both at the places of their martyrdom in Jerusalem and Rome and wherever else Christians met. A thing which had belonged to the martyr could form part of such commemorations. According to the doctrine of the Communion of Saints, martyrs in heaven could intercede for Christians on earth, who needed such advocates at the heavenly court.

Belief in the merits of the Cross, which acted both as the instrument of Christ's victory over death and as the sign of this victory, became widespread in Christian lands. These did not in 569 include the parts of Britain ruled by Saxons. In that year, Venantius Fortunatus welcomed the entry of a relic of the Cross into Poitiers by composing two famous hymns, 'Vexilla regis prodeunt' ('The standards of the king go forth') and 'Pange, lingua' ('Sing, my tongue, the glorious victory'). A century later, the Christian world included Northumbria, where the cult of the Cross became widespread after the Battle of Heavenfield of 633. On the eve of battle, King Oswald of Northumbria had made his army venerate a wooden cross he had set up, and he attributed his victory over pagan Mercia to this veneration. This was a physical re-enactment of the story of Constantine at the Milvian Bridge. Fragments of 1,500 stone preaching crosses survive from early Northumbria. St Cuthbert (d. 687) set up many such crosses. The cross at Ruthwell was made after the return of Bede's abbot from Rome, where in 701 he had witnessed the celebrations following the miraculous discovery by Pope Sergius I of a fragment of the True Cross.

Heavenfield and Ruthwell are not far from Hadrian's Wall, 'with which the Romans formerly enclosed the island from sea to sea', in the words of Bede. Bewcastle, north of the Wall, has a notable stone cross, badly broken but of finer workmanship than that which stands thirty miles to the west at Ruthwell. When King Alfred was in Rome in 885, he was presented with a fragment of the True Cross by Pope Marinus. It is possible that Alfred's fragment is that now in the reliquary in Brussels. It has been suggested that this gift to Alfred may have prompted the expansion of the poem carved in stone at Ruthwell into the longer text in the Vercelli Book.

Cults are open to abuse, and at the height of the Reformation, as at other iconoclastic periods, the cults of relics, of images and of the saints were forbidden. Some Presbyterian churches today disapprove both of images of the crucified Christ and of crosses. Yet the cult of the Cross is biblical: 'May I never boast,' wrote St Paul to some of his converts, 'except of the cross of Our Lord Jesus Christ' (Galatians 6: 14). The hymn 'When I Survey the Wondrous Cross' is sung on Good Friday in Protestant and in Catholic churches. It was composed by the Nonconformist Isaac Watts and published in 1707. Charles Wesley, the founder of Methodism, is reported to have said he would give up all his own hymns to have written this one, which is in the tradition of the sixth-century hymns of Venantius Fortunatus.

The Dream of the Rood is a poem of affective devotion, a common medieval form. The purpose of such poems is to bring an audience, or congregation, into emotional engagement with a Christian truth. It commonly follows the strategy of telling in the first person of an apparently personal experience, often by means of a vision: 'I saw . . .' The vision is initially bewildering, and makes sense only later. This is the genre of many works of medieval literature, such as Dante's *Divine Comedy*, Langland's *Piers Plowman* and the anonymous *Pearl*. In the Old English poem, the Dreamer sees a vision of the Cross, which then speaks to him of its experience at the Crucifixion. An object which speaks is familiar from the riddle tradition (see the previous section on the Exeter Riddles). The Cross speaks as a soldier loyally obeying an unwelcome order from a superior. Loyalty to the lord in battle is central to Old English heroic poetry, as in *The Battle of Maldon*. Here the Cross is an unwilling instrument of its Lord's – its Creator's – death: 'Stand fast I must'. This part of the Rood's speech is like the Gospel accounts of the Crucifixion, except that the Cross initially appears as covered in gold and jewels but then as covered in blood. These aspects alternate constantly. Simultaneous and contrary appearances are part of the riddle tradition, here adapted to the Christian paradox of Christ as simultaneously man and God, defeated and victorious at the same time.

In the early Church, Christ's victory over death was seen as taking place at the Crucifixion, not at the Resurrection. Later in medieval art, the Crucifixion was presented so as to bring out the physical suffering of Jesus, and glory was reserved to the Resurrection. But the figure of Christ in early medieval crucifixions is dignified and impassive, even serene. Likewise, in this poem, the suffering is transferred to the Cross, and Christ is a young hero who strips himself eagerly for the conflict.

After Christ has sent forth his soul, and all Creation has wept, his friends take down the body and bury it in a tomb. The Cross is then buried, along with those of the two thieves, and three lines later (in history, three centuries later) the Cross is discovered. It is then covered in gold and jewels (as fragments of the True Cross were, in reliquaries), and prized as the key to salvation for the faithful. The poem now unfolds the role of the Cross in the redemption of mankind and of the created universe, and ends in a joyful vision of the gathering up of all into heaven at the last day. The more sermon-like second half of the poem is translated into a more literal prose.

The English words carved in runes on the Ruthwell Cross all come from the speech by the Tree, which describes its role in the Crucifixion. This is the core of the poem: the Cross 'speaks'. The Ruthwell Cross was both a symbol and a visual aid. A missionary could speak the words carved on the cross to his unlettered audience, and explain the meaning of the other scenes on the cross. The lines which compose a runic letter are straight, for ease of cutting. They were sometimes incised on the inner side of pieces of bark, to send a message. Trees were sacred in the Germanic pre-Christian religion, and it has been speculated that the audience may have been impressed by the conversion of a stone 'tree' to the new religion. It is clear that the elaborate programme of the sculptural carvings at Ruthwell

is informed by a sophisticated theology, and it has recently been
shown that the design of such a monument is directly influenced
by Christian monuments in Rome.

The Dream of the Rood

Listen!
A dream came to me
        at deep midnight
when humankind
        kept their beds
– the dream of dreams!
        I shall declare it.

It seemed I saw the Tree itself
borne on the air, light wound about it,
– a beam of brightest wood, a beacon clad
in overlapping gold, glancing gems
fair at its foot, and five stones
set in a crux flashed from the crosstree.

Around angels of God
        all gazed upon it,
since first fashioning fair.
        It was not a felon's gallows,
for holy ghosts beheld it there,
and men on mould, and the whole Making shone for it
– *signum* of victory!
                        Stained and marred,
stricken with shame, I saw the glory-tree
shine out gaily, sheathed in yellow
decorous gold; and gemstones made
for their Maker's Tree a right mail-coat.

Yet through the masking gold I might perceive
what terrible sufferings were once sustained thereon:
it bled from the right side.
        Ruth in the heart.

Afraid I saw that unstill brightness
change raiment and colour
        – again clad in gold
or again slicked with sweat,

spangled with spilling blood.

Yet lying there a long while
I beheld, sorrowing, the Healer's Tree
till it seemed that I heard how it broke silence,
best of wood, and began to speak:

'Over that long remove my mind ranges
back to the holt where I was hewn down;
from my own stem I was struck away,
    dragged off by strong enemies,
wrought into a roadside scaffold.
    They made me a hoist for wrongdoers.

The soldiers on their shoulders bore me,
    until on a hill-top they set me up;
many enemies made me fast there.
    Then I saw, marching toward me,
mankind's brave King;
    He came to climb upon me.

I dared not break or bend aside
against God's will, though the ground itself
shook at my feet. Fast I stood,
who falling could have felled them all.

Almighty God ungirded Him,
    eager to mount the gallows,
unafraid in the sight of many:
    He would set free mankind.
I shook when His arms embraced me
    but I durst not bow to ground,
stoop to Earth's surface.
    Stand fast I must.

I was reared up, a rood.
    I raised the great King,
liege lord of the heavens,
    dared not lean from the true.

They drove me through with dark nails:
　　on me are the deep wounds manifest,
wide-mouthed hate-dents.
　　　　I durst not harm any of them.
How they mocked at us both!
　　　　I was all moist with blood
sprung from the Man's side
　　　　after He sent forth His soul.

Wry wierds a-many I underwent
up on that hill-top; saw the Lord of Hosts
stretched out stark. Darkness shrouded
the King's corse. Clouds wrapped
its clear shining. A shade went out
wan under cloud-pall. All creation wept,
keened the King's death. Christ was on the Cross.

But there quickly came from far
earls to the One there. All that I beheld,
had grown weak with grief,
　　　　yet with glad will bent then
meek to those men's hands,
　　　　yielded Almighty God.

They lifted Him down from the leaden pain,
　　　　left me, the commanders,
standing in a sweat of blood.
　　　　I was all wounded with shafts.

They straightened out His strained limbs,
　　　　stood at His body's head,
looked down on the Lord of Heaven
　　　　– for a while He lay there resting –
set to contrive Him a tomb
　　　　in the sight of the Tree of Death,
carved it of bright stone,
　　　　laid in it the Bringer of Victory,
spent from the great struggle.
　　　　They began to speak the grief-song,

sad in the sinking light,
    then thought to set out homeward;
their hearts were sick to death,
    their most high Prince
they left to rest there with scant retinue.

Yet we three, weeping, a good while
stood in that place after the song had gone up
from the captains' throats. Cold grew the corse,
fair soul-house.
             They felled us all.
We crashed to ground, cruel Wierd,
and they delved for us a deep pit.

The Lord's men learned of it,
His friends found me . . .
it was they who girt me with gold and silver . . .

[78–156]
'Now, my dear man, you may understand that I have suffered
to the end the pain of grievous sorrows at the hands of dwellers
in misery. The time is now come that men on earth, and all this
marvellous creation, shall honour me far and wide and address
themselves in prayer to this sign. On me the Son of God spent
a time of suffering. Therefore do I now tower up glorious
beneath the heavens, and I have the power to save every man
who fears me. Formerly I was made the worst of punishments,
the most hateful to the peoples – before I opened to men, the
speech-bearers, the right way to life.

Behold, the Prince of Glory then exalted me above the trees
of the forest, the Keeper of the Kingdom of Heaven; just as He
also, Almighty God, for the sake of all mankind, exalted His
mother, Mary herself, above all womankind.

I now command you, my dear man, to tell men about
this sight, reveal in words that this is the tree of glory on
which Almighty God suffered for the many sins of man-
kind and Adam's deeds of old. He tasted death thereupon; yet

afterwards the Lord rose up, to help men with His great might. Then He went up to the heavens. Hither He shall come again to seek out mankind on the day of doom, the Lord Himself, Almighty God, and with Him His angels, when He then will adjudge – Who has the power of judgement – to each and every one according to how he shall formerly have deserved for himself here in this transitory life. Nor can anyone there be unconcerned about the word that the Ruler shall utter. He shall ask before the multitude, Where is the man who is willing to taste bitter death for the Lord's name's sake? – as He had formerly done on the tree. But they shall then be afraid, and few shall think what they shall begin to answer to Christ. Yet no one there shall need to be afraid who has borne in his bosom the best of signs. But every soul on earth who intends to dwell with the Lord shall come to the Kingdom through the Rood.'

Then I prayed to the tree with cheerful heart and high zeal, alone as I was and with small retinue. My spirit was drawn forth on its way hence; in all it had endured many times of longing. The hope of my life is now that I should seek out that tree of victory, alone and more frequently than all men, to worship it fully. The desire to do this is strong in my mind, and my hope of protection is all bent on the Rood. I have not many powerful friends on earth. On the contrary, they have departed hence out of the world's joys, have sought out the King of Glory and live now in the heavens with the Almighty Father, dwelling in glory; and every day I look for the time when the Lord's Rood, which once I gazed on here on earth, shall fetch me forth from this fleeting life and then shall bring me where there is great rejoicing, happiness in the heavens, where the Lord's people is seated at the feast, where there is bliss everlasting; and then He shall appoint me to a place where after I may dwell in glory, and fully share in joy among the blest.

May the Lord be my friend, who here on earth once suffered on the gallows tree for the sins of man. He ransomed us and gave us life, a heavenly home. Hope was made new, with glory and with bliss, for those who had suffered burning there. The Son was victorious on that expedition,* mighty and triumphant, when He came, the Almighty Sovereign, with a multitude, a host of spirits, into God's Kingdom, to the bliss of the angels and all of the saints who had previously dwelt in glory, when their Ruler came, Almighty God, into His own Kingdom.

*The Harrowing of Hell

TWO OLD ENGLISH POEMS

Readers may wish to see some Old English. Two early exhibits are *Cædmon's Hymn* (before 680) and *Bede's Death Song* (735). These fourteen lines are all that remains of the English verse of Cædmon and Bede; not a line of St Aldhelm's poetry has survived. Cædmon is known to us from the pages of Bede's *Historia ecclesiastica gentis Anglorum*, a Christian history of the English people completed in 731. Bede tells us that Cædmon was a layman who joined the monastery at Whitby Abbey late in life. Whitby was a double monastery, for both women and men, under the Abbess Hilda. It was the custom, Bede says, at an evening party for everyone to recite verses to the harp; poetry was often accompanied by music. Cædmon did not know how to recite, and when he saw the harp coming near to him, he would leave the feast and walk back to his house. One night he left the group and, having visited the cattle pens, his task for the night, went to bed as usual. There he dreamed that a certain man stood by him who said: 'Cædmon, sing me something.' Cædmon replied that he did not know how to sing and that that was why he had left the party. 'Yet you can sing to me,' replied the visitor. 'What shall I sing?' asked Cædmon. 'Sing me the beginning of created things.' When Cædmon had received this answer, he immediately began to sing verses in praise of God the Creator which he had never heard before. Bede's Latin text continues with a literal paraphrase of Cædmon's hymn of Creation.

No fewer than 160 manuscript copies of Bede's Latin *History* survive. Old English versions of the *Hymn* have been written in the margins of some copies. Twenty-three copies of the *Hymn* survive, in five different versions. This makes it the best-attested poetic text, except for *Bede's Death Song*, which follows next. The Moore manuscript, now in Cambridge, was written within a few years of Bede's death in 735. Its text of the *Hymn* is in the Northumbrian dialect, and may come from Bede's monastery.

Cædmon's Hymn

    Nu scylun hergan   hefaenricaes uard,
    metudæs maecti   end his modgidanc,
    uerc uuldurfadur,   sue he uundra gihuaes,
    eci dryctin,   or astelidæ.
5   He aerist scop   aelda barnum
    heben til hrofe,   haleg scepen;
    tha middungeard   moncynnæs uard,
    eci dryctin,   æfter tiadæ,
    firum foldu,   frea allmectig.

The second text is in a Late West Saxon manuscript of the eleventh century. Among the differences are *eorthan* (of earth) for *aelda* (of men) in line 5.

    Nu we sculan herian   heofonrices Weard,
    Metodes mihte   and his modgeþonc,
    weorc Wuldorfæder;   swa he wundra gehwæs,
    ece Dryhten,   ord onstealde.
5   He ærest gesceop   eorðan bearnum
    heofon to hrofe,   halig Scyppend:
    ða middongeard   moncynnes Weard,
    ece Dryhten,   æfter teode
    firum foldan,   Frea ælmihtig.

The following version translates the West Saxon text:

    Praise now to the keeper of the kingdom of heaven,
    the power of the Creator, the profound mind
    of the glorious Father, who fashioned the beginning

of every wonder, the eternal Lord.
5   For the children of men He made first
heaven as a roof, the holy Creator.
Then the Lord of mankind, the everlasting
    Shepherd,
ordained in the midst as a dwelling place,
Almighty Lord, the earth for men.

After Bede had died in 735, his disciple Cuthbert wrote in a letter that the dying man had sung the verse of St Paul the Apostle telling of the fearfulness of falling into the hands of the living God (Hebrews 10: 31). Cuthbert adds that Bede had sung 'in our language also, as he was learned in our songs, speaking of the terrible departure of spirits from the body'. Cuthbert then gives the text in its original Northumbrian.

Bede's Death Song

Fore thaem neidfaerae   naenig uuirthit
thoncsnotturra,   than him tharf sie
to ymbhycggannae aer   his hiniongae
hwaet his gastae   godaes aeththae yflaes
aefter deothdaege   doemid uueorthae.

A literal prose version of this might be:

Before that sudden journey no one is wiser in thought than he needs to be, in considering, before his departure, what will be adjudged to his soul, of good or evil, after his death-day.

'No one is wiser in thought than he needs to be' expresses, in a classically negative form, a typical Anglo-Saxon attitude to life as well as to death.

ELEGIES

Many of the shorter poems of the Exeter Book were grouped together as 'elegies'. All voice feelings of sadness, but some place loss in a framework of Christian consolation, and others could equally be described as love poems. 'Elegies' is now little more than a label for a group of dramatically voiced poems whose direct expression of emotion has appealed to post-Romantic taste.

THE WANDERER and THE SEAFARER

These are perhaps the best-known shorter poems in Old English. Near neighbours in the Exeter Book, the poems have similar concerns, and present no major difficulties in interpretation. They form a natural pair, and the opportunity to compare them is especially welcome.

Comparison of closely similar texts is otherwise possible only with the Exeter Riddles and with the verse paraphrases of Scripture. The chief context for a text is often the manuscript in which it is found, there being no external evidence for how the text got into the manuscript, where the manuscript came from, its authorship, date and place of composition, patron or audience. Points of reference outside the text are scarce. Of the poets with known names, Cædmon and Bede left no more than *Cædmon's Hymn* and *Bede's Death Song* – fourteen lines in all. The poet who signed four long poems 'Cynewulf' so that we might pray for him is otherwise unknown. The *Anglo-Saxon Chronicle* allows two poems to be dated firmly: the entry for

937 consists of the poem on the battle at Brunanburgh, though the place cannot be identified. The annal for 991 records a battle at Maldon, about which there is a fine poem, though this survives incompletely and in a transcript of 1725. Art history points to the probable date for the carving of the verse inscription on the Ruthwell Cross as the early 700s. Manuscripts too can be dated within twenty years, but the composition of the poems they contain cannot. Although *Beowulf* is said to have attracted more learned articles than *Hamlet*, we do not know who wrote it, when, where or for what audience. It is not known whether Beowulf was a real person. An eighth-century composition seems likely, but scholars have seriously proposed the seventh and every other Saxon century, even the eleventh. Since, then, most poetic texts lack contexts, it is good that two poems in the same manuscript offer mutual illumination.

The Wanderer and *The Seafarer* address human destinies, individual and general. The voice of an unspecified speaker reflects gravely or passionately upon the experience of exile and loss of kindred, and then upon the fates of human societies, and finally on the end of the individual person. This was a new theme for a poetic tradition whose origins were oral, whose habitual address was social and which had been used to strengthen the bonds of mutual service between lord and man in case of war. The Wanderer figure and the Seafarer figure (these titles, we should bear in mind, were bestowed in the nineteenth century) speak at first autobiographically, but later more generally. The personal experience which authenticates the voice lends power to the moving moral reflections that dominate the latter stages of each poem. Gnomic reflection, an established mode of Germanic poetry, moves into something more explicitly Christian, especially in *The Seafarer*.

The punctuation of Old English texts does not include speech marks. Editions differ as to where the two speeches, or trains of thought, which make up most of the text of *The Wanderer* begin and end. But a move from the personal to the general is clear, and the first line and a half are carefully answered in the last line and a half, confirming that such a widening of focus towards universals is the strategy of the poem. *The Seafarer* is

less sober and more radical: an anguished speaker deprived of
kinsmen contrasts the comfortable life of settled communities
on land with the life of a solitary seafarer; the speaker has
chosen this harder life.

Both poems face the same question. When lord, kindred and
friends are dead, when society is gone, what is the fate of the
individual? *The Wanderer* concludes that lasting security is to
be found only with the Father in heaven. It moves forward
methodically in the direction pointed by Boethius in *The Conso-
lation of Philosophy*, a work translated by King Alfred. *The
Seafarer* takes a more erratic depths-and-heights route to a
more ecstatic and Christian end. Like *The Ruin*, these poems
contemplate ruined cities. Like *The Dream of the Rood*, they
take the speaker and the audience from a stricken and solitary
state towards a philosophical and heavenly resolution.

The anguish of the speeches early in each poem may have
suggested these titles to nineteenth-century editors: titles used
by German Romantic poets and composers. The poems engage
the reader (it is easier to imagine a reader than an audience) by
their apparent origin in personal experience. But they are fictive
dramatic monologues designed to make the reader think
beyond the present, and learn, not without pain and longing
for what has gone, the hard lessons of an ancient wisdom. The
second speaker in the second part of *The Wanderer* is not a lost
soul brimming with *Weltschmerz* but a Ponderer in the manner
of Boethius. Boethius (AD 480–524) was a Roman patrician, a
distinguished exponent of Platonic and Stoic philosophy, and
a statesman. He had served as consul, the highest position under
the emperor. In the year in which both his sons became consuls,
the philosopher was thrown into prison by the Roman emperor
Theodoric for reasons now obscure, though the emperor was a
Goth and an Arian, and Boethius a Catholic. In the year 524,
Theodoric had Boethius tortured to death, but not before he
had written a series of dialogues in which Lady Philosophy
eventually consoles him for the reversal of his worldly fortunes
by arguments which convince him that the injustices of our
present life are masks of divine justice, and that eternal re-
wards await wisdom and virtue. Although a Christian, Boethius

THE WANDERER AND THE SEAFARER

makes Philosophy argue from Reason not Revelation. His *Consolation* is the philosophical equivalent of the Book of Job. It became the most popular book of the Latin Middle Ages, with the exception of the Vulgate Bible and some writings of St Augustine of Hippo and, in England, of Gregory the Great. The *Consolation* was translated by Alfred, by Chaucer and by Elizabeth I, and preserved its reputation as a 'golden volume' throughout the Enlightenment.

The headnote to *The Ruin* mentioned the effect of the Fall of Rome on the Christian West, as seen in Augustine's *City of God*. The Rome which had destroyed Jerusalem had itself suffered destruction. The image of the ruined city reappears in both *The Wanderer* and *The Seafarer*. In the twentieth century, Old English scholarship overcame its nativist tendencies and gradually familiarized itself with the abundant literary remains of the Christian Latin culture of Saxon England. Both poems echo biblical texts which lament the destruction of Jerusalem, and the homelessness of man's soul on earth. *The Wanderer* begins '*Oft se anhaga are gebideth*': 'Often the solitary man longs for (*or* lives to experience) mercy'. *Oft* is a poetic understatement meaning 'always'. *Anhaga* means 'one who lives alone'; among the equivalents of this word is *monachos*, monk. *The Seafarer* belongs in part to the tradition of *peregrinatio pro amore Dei*: 'voluntary exile for the love of God'. This was the impulse which took St Antony and other ascetics into the Egyptian desert, Columba to Iona, Cuthbert to Lindisfarne and the warrior prince Guthlac to Crowland, an island in the Fens: the lonely impulse which inspired generations of Celtic monks to seek uninhabited places like Skellig Michael and other rocks off the west coast of Ireland: 'a far homeland flood-beyond', nearer to our heavenly home. This is not a legend, like the *Voyage of St Brendan*, but a well-recorded historical movement which founded a score of monasteries still standing across Europe. A local instance is recorded in the *Anglo-Saxon Chronicle* for the year 891:

Three Irishmen came to King Alfred in a boat without any oars, from Ireland, whence they had stolen away because they wished

for the love of God to be on pilgrimage, they cared not where.
The boat in which they set out was made of two and a half hides,
and they had taken with them provisions for a week and after a
week they came to land in Cornwall, and soon came to King
Alfred.

Just as *The Wanderer* needs to be seen against the back-
ground of the thought of Christian late antiquity as voiced
by Boethius, so *The Seafarer* expresses a distinctly religious
impulse to withdraw from this world.

The Wanderer

Who liveth alone longeth for mercy,
Maker's mercy. Though he must traverse
tracts of sea, sick at heart
– trouble with oars ice-cold waters,
the ways of exile – Wierd is set fast.

Thus spoke such a 'grasshopper', old griefs in his mind,
cold slaughters, the death of dear kinsmen:

'Alone am I driven each day before daybreak
to give my cares utterance.
None are there now among the living
to whom I dare declare me throughly,
tell my heart's thought. Too truly I know
it is in a man no mean virtue
that he keep close his heart's chest,
hold his thought-hoard, think as he may.

No weary mind may stand against Wierd
nor may a wrecked will work new hope;
wherefore, most often, those eager for fame
bind the dark mood fast in their breasts.

So must I also curb my mind,
cut off from country, from kind far distant,
by cares overworn, bind it in fetters;
this since, long ago, the ground's shroud
enwrapped my gold-friend. Wretched I went thence,
winter-wearied, over the waves' bound;
dreary I sought hall of a gold-giver,
where far or near I might find
him who in mead-hall might take heed of me,
furnish comfort to a man friendless,
win me with cheer.
                    He knows who makes trial
how harsh and bitter is care for companion

to him who hath few friends to shield him.
Track ever taketh him, never the torqued gold,
not earthly glory, but cold heart's cave.
He minds him of hall-men, of treasure-giving,
how in his youth his gold-friend
gave him to feast. Fallen all this joy.

He knows this who is forced to forgo his lord's,
his friend's counsels, to lack them for long:
oft sorrow and sleep, banded together,
come to bind the lone outcast;
he thinks in his heart then that he his lord
claspeth and kisseth, and on knee layeth
hand and head, as he had at otherwhiles
in days now gone, when he enjoyed the gift-stool.

Awakeneth after this friendless man,
seeth before him fallow waves,
seabirds bathing, broading out feathers,
snow and hail swirl, hoar-frost falling.
Then all the heavier his heart's wounds,
sore for his loved lord. Sorrow freshens.

Remembered kinsmen press through his mind;
he singeth out gladly, scanneth eagerly
men from the same hearth. They swim away.
Sailors' ghosts bring not many
known songs there. Care grows fresh
in him who shall send forth too often
over locked waves his weary spirit.

Therefore I may not think, throughout this world,
why cloud cometh not on my mind
when I think over all the life of earls,
how at a stroke they have given up hall,
mood-proud thanes. So this middle earth
each of all days ageth and falleth.'

Wherefore no man grows wise without he have
his share of winters. A wise man holds out;
he is not too hot-hearted, nor too hasty in speech,
nor too weak a warrior, not wanting in fore-thought,
nor too greedy of goods, nor too glad, nor too mild,
nor ever too eager to boast, ere he knows all.

A man should forbear boastmaking
until his fierce mind fully knows
which way his spleen shall expend itself.

A wise man may grasp how ghastly it shall be
when all this world's wealth standeth waste,
even as now, in many places, over the earth
walls stand, wind-beaten,
hung with hoar-frost; ruined habitations.
The wine-halls crumble; their wielders lie
bereft of bliss, the band all fallen
proud by the wall. War took off some,
carried them on their course hence; one a bird bore
over the high sea; one the hoar wolf
dealt to death; one his drear-cheeked
earl stretched in an earthen trench.

The Maker of men hath so marred this dwelling
that human laughter is not heard about it
and idle stand these old giant-works.
A man who on these walls wisely looked
who sounded deeply this dark life
would think back to the blood spilt here,
weigh it in his wit. His word would be this:
'Where is that horse now? Where are those men?
        Where is the hoard-sharer?
Where is the house of the feast? Where is the hall's
        uproar?

    Alas, bright cup! Alas, burnished fighter!
    Alas, proud prince! How that time has passed,
    dark under night's helm, as though it never had
        been!

There stands in the stead of staunch thanes
a towering wall wrought with worm-shapes;
the earls are off-taken by the ash-spear's point
– that thirsty weapon. Their Wierd is glorious.

Storms break on the stone hillside,
the ground bound by driving sleet,
winter's wrath. Then wanness cometh,
night's shade spreadeth, sendeth from north
the rough hail to harry mankind.

In the earth-realm all is crossed;
Wierd's will changeth the world.
Wealth is lent us, friends are lent us,
man is lent, kin is lent;
all this earth's frame shall stand empty.'

So spoke the sage in his heart; he sat apart in thought.
Good is he who keeps faith: nor should care too fast
be out of a man's breast before he first know the cure:
a warrior fights on bravely. Well is it for him who
          seeks forgiveness,
the Heavenly Father's solace, in whom all our fastness
          stands.

The Seafarer

The tale I frame shall be found to tally:
the history is of myself.
                              Sitting day-long
at an oar's end clenched against clinging sorrow,
breast-drought I have borne, and bitternesses too.
I have coursed my keel through care-halls without end
over furled foam, I forward in the bows
through the narrowing night, numb, watching
for the cliffs we beat along.
                              Cold then
nailed my feet, frost shrank on
its chill clamps, cares sighed
hot about heart, hunger fed
on a mere-wearied mind.
                              No man blessed
with a happy land-life is like to guess
how I, aching-hearted, on ice-cold seas
have wasted whole winters; the wanderer's beat,
cut off from kind. . . .
hung with hoar-frost.
                              Hail flew in showers,
there was no sound there but the slam of waves
along an icy sea. The swan's blare
my seldom amusement; for men's laughter
there was curlew-call, there were the cries of gannets,
for mead-drinking the music of the gull.
To the storm striking the stone cliffs
gull would answer, eagle scream
from throats frost-feathered. No friend or brother
by to speak with the despairing mind.

This he little believes whose life has run
sweet in the burghs, no banished man,
but well-seen at wine-round, my weariness of mind
on the ways stretching over the salt plains.

Night thickened, and from the north snowflakes;
hail fell on the frost-bound earth,
coldest of grains.

                There come thoughts now
knocking my heart, of the high waves,
clashing salt-crests, I am to cross again.
Mind-lust maddens, moves as I breathe
soul to set out, seek out the way
to a far folk-land flood-beyond.

For no man above mould is so mood-proud,
so thoroughly equipped, so quick to do,
so strong in his youth, or with so staunch a lord
that before faring on the sea he does not fear a little
whither the Lord shall lead him in the end.
His heart is not in harping nor in the having of rings,
has no delight in women nor the world's gladnesses
nor can think of any thing outside the thrash of waves,
sea-struck, is distracted, stillness lost.

The thriving of the treeland, the town's briskness,
a lightness over the leas, life gathering,
everything urges the eagerly mooded
man to venture on the voyage he thinks of,
the faring over flood, the far bourn.
And the cuckoo calls him in his care-laden voice,
scout of summer, sings of new griefs
that shall make breast-hoard bitter.
                       Blithe heart cannot know,
through its happiness, what hardships they suffer
who drive the foam-furrow furthest from land.
Spirit breaks from the body's chest
to the sea's acres; over earth's breadth
and whale's range roams the mind now,
homes to the breast hungry and thirsty.

Cuckoo's dirge drags out my heart,
whets will to the whale's beat
across wastes of water: far warmer to me
are the Lord's kindnesses than this life of death
lent us on land.
            I do not believe
earthly estate is everlasting:
three things all ways threaten a man's peace
and one before the end shall overthrow his mind;
either illness or age or the edge of vengeance
shall draw out the breath from the doom-shadowed.
Wherefore, for earl whosoever, it is afterword,
the praise of livers-on, that, lasting, is best:
won in the world before wayfaring,
forged, framed here, in the face of enmity,
in the Devil's spite: deeds, achievements.
That after-speakers should respect the name
and after them angels have honour towards it
for always and ever. From those everlasting joys
the daring shall not die.
                  Days are soon over,
on earth imperium with the earl's hand fails;
kings are not now, kaisers are not,
there are no gold-givers like the gone masters
who between them framed the first deeds in the world,
in their lives lordly, in the lays renowned.
That chivalry is changed, cheer is gone away,
it is a weaker kind who wields earth now,
sweats for its bread. Brave men are fewer,
all excellence on earth grows old and sere
as now does every man over the world;
age fares against him, his face bleaches
and his thatch thins: had a throng of friends
of noble houses, knows now they all
are given to the ground. That grieves his white head.
Once life is going, this gristle slackens;
nothing can pain or please flesh then,

he cannot stir a finger, fix his thinking.
A man may bury his brother with the dead
and strew his grave with the golden things
he would have him take, treasures of all kinds,
but gold hoarded when he here lived
cannot allay the anger of God
towards a soul sin-freighted.

[103–24]

Great is the terrible power of God, before which the earth shall
turn aside; He established the firm foundations, the expanse of
the earth, the heavens above. Foolish is the man who does not
fear his Lord; death shall come upon him unprepared. Blessed
is the man who lives in trust; grace shall come to him from the
heavens. The Lord shall confirm that spirit in him, for he
believes in His might. A man should manage a headstrong spirit
and keep it in its place, and be true to men, fair in his dealings.
He should treat every man with measure, restrain enmity
towards friend and foe. He may not wish his cherished friend
to be given over to the fire nor to be burned on the pyre,
yet Doom is stronger and God is mightier than any man's
conception. Let us think where it is that we may find a home
and then consider how we may come thither, and then indeed
we may strive so that we may be able to enter into that everlast-
ing blessedness where all life is in the Lord's love, the bliss of
heaven. Thanks be to the Holy One therefore, the Prince of
Glory, the everlasting Lord, that He has raised us up forever.
Amen.

LOVE POEMS

Beowulf and *The Battle of Maldon* – and *The Dream of the Rood* – tell us that man is doomed to die and must face death undismayed. This is the famous note of Old English poetry, though there is more even to the battle poems than this, and very much more to *Beowulf*. Yet fate and fatalism bulk large in the received idea of Old English poetry. Most of what survives is Christian and full of hope, but the history of the reception of Old English shows that it has been the heroic poems and 'elegies' which have engaged modern readers. Some readers, indeed, wanted their past not to be historically Saxon but pre-historically pagan: fur and feather, blood and doom.

It is true of the heroic poems that they presuppose a society formed by the needs of war, a hard world which prized loyalty, courage, skill and judgement. As late as *The Battle of Maldon* (991+), the man who left a battlefield on which his lord lay dead should not return home but live in exile and disgrace. There are no women in the battle poems, but women play significant parts in the heroic poems, especially in *Beowulf*. *Elene* is a long poem about a woman's achievements, as is *Judith*, the other poem in the *Beowulf* manuscript. The heroine's name means 'Jewess', and this representative of the Jewish nation uses her beauty and her brains to save it from its enemies.

Most Old English poems are not about love between men and women, but women are central to all three love poems in this section, two of which voice the woman's feelings. (There are a number of such poems in medieval literature, some written by women.) The poems known as *The Ruin, The Wanderer* and *The Seafarer* have been given generic titles, as have *The Wife's Lament* and *The Husband's Message*. This seems appropriate, for none of these poems includes a personal name: the situations and sentiments of the poems are typical rather than historical. This applies also to *Wulf and Eadwacer*, for Wulf and Eadwacer are not known to history, unlike most of the names in the heroic poems, *Deor* and *Widsith*.

The Wife's Lament, *The Husband's Message* and *Wulf and Eadwacer* form a distinct sub-set among the shorter poems usually grouped together as elegies. These three love poems consist of dramatic and often emotional speeches. In each the scenario is unspecified and has to be worked out. The implied situation seems to be familiar and generic: the abandoned wife, the husband impatient to rejoin his wife, the lovers separated by an unwelcome marriage and by feud. Modern editors reconstruct these implied situations, though the reconstructions differ. In any case, these poems are more enigmatic to us than they would have been to their original audiences. When selections of Old English poems were first drawn up for study, there was a preference for texts whose problems had known solutions. Readers of poetry today are more used to the enigmatic.

THE WIFE'S LAMENT

In this edition, the title *The Wife's Lament* has replaced the less dignified *The Wife's Complaint*. The speaker is in exile, banished by a husband who has been misled by false report. She lives in a cave beneath an oak tree, far from the man she loves. She curses a second man who has brought about this estrangement, and imagines her husband on a distant and hostile shore. The poem ends with the kind of weighty reflection forced out by experience which opens both *The Wanderer* and *The Seafarer*, and was deeply appreciated by the audience of its time. This powerful and dramatic poem reads as autobiography but is fictional. It has themes familiar in medieval literature. The use of a woman's voice to express grief is found in Latin verse and at Beowulf's funeral; the breaking-up of a marriage by jealous kinsmen recurs in two places in *Beowulf*; the wintry landscape of loss is paralleled in *The Wanderer*'s vision of the end of the world; and despair beneath an oak tree is found twice in Chaucer. Yet this remains perhaps the most intense and distinctive of the Old English elegies.

The Wife's Lament

I have wrought these words together out of a wryed
    existence,
the heart's tally, telling off
the griefs I have undergone from girlhood upwards,
old and new, and now more than ever;
for I have never not had some new sorrow,
some fresh affliction to fight against.

The first was my lord's leaving his people here:
crossed crests. To what country I knew not,
wondered where, awoke unhappy.
I left, fared any road, friendless, an outcast,
sought any service to staunch the lack of him.

Then his kinsmen ganged, began to think
thoughts they did not speak, of splitting the wedlock;
so – estranged, alienated – we lived each
alone, a long way apart; how I longed for him!

In his harshness he had me brought here;
and in these parts there were few friendly minded,
worth trusting.
              Trouble in the heart now:
I saw the bitterness, the bound mind
of my matched man, mourning-browed,
mirk in his mood, murder in his thoughts.

Our lips had smiled to swear hourly
that nothing should split us – save dying –
nothing else. All that has changed:
it is now as if it never had been,
our friendship. I feel in the wind
that the man dearest to me detests me.
I was banished to this knoll knotted by woods
to live in a den dug beneath an oak.
Old is this earthen room; it eats at my heart.

I see the thorns thrive up there in thick coverts
on the banks that baulk these black hollows:
not a gay dwelling. Here the grief bred
by lordlack preys on me. Some lovers in this world
live dear to each other, lie warm together
at day's beginning; I go by myself
about these earth caves under the oak tree.
Here I must sit the summer day through,
here weep out the woes of exile,
the hardships heaped upon me. My heart shall never
suddenly sail into slack water,
all the longings of a lifetime answered.

May grief and bitterness blast the mind
of that young man! May his mind ache
behind his smiling face! May a flock of sorrows
choke his chest! He would change his tune
if he lived alone in a land of exile
far from his folk.
                      Where my friend is stranded
frost crusts the cracked cliff-face,
grey waves grind the shingle.
The mind cannot bear in such a bleak place
very much grief.
                      He remembers too often
less grim surroundings. Sorrow follows
this too long wait for one who is estranged.

THE HUSBAND'S MESSAGE

The Husband's Message, which comes a few pages later in the Exeter Book, is not part of the same story, despite its editorial title. It shares the theme of separation found in most of the elegies, and the lovers in the poem are separated, as in the other two love poems. Unlike most of the surviving literature, it is courtly, almost chivalric, and expresses hope, not sadness.

The message of the title is spoken by the staff upon which the sender's words are carved: 'Now shall I unseal myself to yourself alone.' The idea of an object speaking is familiar from the Exeter Riddles; see especially the Reed or Papyrus riddle (number 60, p. 26). The text of the poem is the message. It ends with a runic token, discussed in A Note on Runes. (The root meaning of Old English *rūn* is 'secret' or 'secret message'. A Middle English lyric refers to the song of birds as *briddès rūn*.) The old Germanic runic alphabet consisted of straight-sided characters designed to be cut on wood, as here. Since the staff is itself a kind of token between the lovers, the cryptic associations of runic writing suit the occasion. *Wrītan*, the Old English word for 'to write', originally meant 'to incise'.

The text of the poem is broken almost immediately by the burn marks which have affected several leaves towards the back of the Exeter Book, yet the direction of the sense remains clear. The wood tells how it grew in a foreign land and is now sent by ship to bring its message. It reminds the lady of the promises made before the couple were separated by a feud and he had to leave their homeland. The husband asks her to make ready to come to him in the spring, leaving as soon as she hears the cuckoo call. He has prospered in his new home, where they can be happy together. He concludes by reminding her of their promise, and delivers the final secret token. The audience may have known the story and whether this hope was fulfilled. If so, this is a further correction to the idea of Old English poetry as doomladen.

The Husband's Message

Now shall I unseal myself to yourself alone
. . . the wood kind, waxed from saplinghood;
on me . . .   must in foreign lands
set . . .
saltstreams.
                    In the beak of ships
I have often been
where my lord . . .   me
among high houses; and here am come now
on board a ship.
                    You shall directly
know how you may think of the thorough love
my lord feels for you. I have no fear in promising
you shall find him heart-whole, honour bright.

Hwæt!
        The carver of this token entreats a lady
clad in clear stones to call to mind
and hold in her wit words pledged
often between the two in earlier days:
then he would hand you through hall and yard
lord of his lands, and you might live together,
forge your love. A feud drove him
from his war-proud people.
                        That prince, glad now,
gave me this word for you: when you shall hear
in the copse at the cliff's edge the cuckoo pitch
his melancholy cry, come over sea.

You will have listened long: leave then with no notice,
let no man alive delay your going:
into the boat and out to sea,
the seagull's range; southward from here
over the paths in the foam you shall find your man,
make landfall where your lord is waiting.

He does not conceive, he said to me,
that a greater happiness could be his in this world
than that all-wielding God should grant you both
days when together you may give out rings
among followers and fellows, free-handed deal
the nailed armbands. Of which he has enough,
of inlaid gold . . .

There lands are his, a hearth among strangers,
estate . . .
                . . . of men,
although my lord here . . .
when the need grew strait, steered his boat out
through steep breakers, and had singlehanded
to run the deep ways, dared escape,
mingled saltstreams. The man has now
laid his sorrows, lacks no gladdeners;
he has a hoard and horses and hall-carousing
and would have everything within an earl's having
had he my lady with him: if my lady will come:
if she will hold to what was sworn and sealed in your
                youths.

So I set together, S and R twinned,
E A, W, D. The oath is named
whereby he undertakes until the end of his life
to keep the covenants of companionship
that, long ago, you delighted to repeat.

WULF AND EADWACER

This poem follows *Deor* in the Exeter Book. Its story cannot be identified, but like *Deor* it seems to belong to an unbaptized Germanic world. It too is strophic in form: groups of verses are followed by a refrain. Other Old English verse runs continuously in the standard metre. W. H. Auden included this translation of *Wulf and Eadwacer* in his personal anthology *A Certain World* (1970), and he also included the translation of *Deor*, which heads the next section. Both of these poems are like some of the poems of the Old Icelandic *Eddas*, which Auden translated with the help of an Old Norse scholar. He was a poet who liked the compressed and the enigmatic, qualities found also in the heroic allusions of *Deor*, *Widsith* and *Beowulf*. After the first two strophes, the poem changes its verse form and then changes it again.

The story of the poem was cracked in 1888 by Henry Bradley, who in 1915 succeeded James Murray as editor of what is now called the *Oxford English Dictionary*. Bradley advances his solution with a lexicographer's precision: 'The speaker, it should be premised, is shown by the grammar to be a woman, Wulf is her lover and an outlaw, and Eadwacer (I suspect, though it is not certain) is her tyrant husband.'

In the penultimate sentence, the 'whelp' she speaks of is her child, but, as the word suggests, the father is not her husband, Eadwacer, but Wulf.

Wulf and Eadwacer

The men of my tribe would treat him as game:
if he comes to the camp they will kill him outright.

    Our fate is forked.

Wulf is on one island, I on another.
Mine is a fastness: the fens girdle it
and it is defended by the fiercest men.
If he comes to the camp they will kill him for sure.

    Our fate is forked.

It was rainy weather, and I wept by the hearth,
thinking of my Wulf's far wanderings;
one of the captains caught me in his arms.
It gladdened me then; but it grieved me too.

Wulf, my Wulf, it was wanting you
that made me sick, your seldom coming,
the hollowness at heart; not the hunger I spoke of.

Do you hear, Eadwacer? Our whelp
    Wulf shall take to the wood.
What was never bound is broken easily,
    our song together.

HEROIC POEMS

Heroic poetry is set in a legendary past inhabited by historical heroes whose exploits and virtues are idealized, as in *Deor*, *Beowulf*, *The Battle of Finnsburgh* and *Widsith*. It also includes poems on historical battles, such as those at Brunanburgh and at Maldon, in tenth-century England: poems in which the ethical criteria of the heroic age are applied to the conduct of warriors in battle.

DEOR

Deor, it is revealed towards the end of the poem, is the speaker. The name is also a general term for a wild animal, not narrowed to the modern meaning of 'deer'. Deor is a poet, and his name is like that of the poet-speaker of *Widsith*, a name which itself means Far-Venture(r), Traveller. Both Deor and Widsith are itinerant singers who go from court to court. Widsith travels across Europe from north-west to south-east, visiting the courts of Germanic heroes famous in history and legend, and also to the court of Attila the Hun. The functions of an oral poet included praise of the patron, the raising of morale, and general remembrancer: preserving the tale of the tribe and all that it needed to know. *Widsith*, which can be found at the end of this section, consists largely of lists of the peoples of greater Germania and their neighbours, with flashes of narrative.

Deor, by contrast, has more concentration and shape than any of the shorter poems except *Wulf and Eadwacer*, which it resembles in that both begin with strophes, groups of verses followed by a refrain. *Deor* keeps to this pattern until the end; the six strophes vary in length, the last being much the longest. The refrain runs '*Thæs ofereode, thisses swa mæg*': 'That went by; this may too'. This is followed each time by a space left in the manuscript, while the '*ungelic is us*' of *Wulf and Eadwacer* has no space after it.

A periodic and punctuated form suits the purpose of *Deor*, which consists of a series of cruel acts of oppression overcome or outlived. These wrongs are taken first from legend and then from history, before the narrative finally turns to the poet himself and his own misfortune. The full sense of the refrain is difficult to express in modern English. The sense could be contortedly construed as follows: 'It passed over in respect of that. May it likewise pass over in respect of this!'

The first strophe tells of the exile of Wayland, the smith of the Northern gods, captured and hamstrung by Nithhad. The second shows Wayland's savage vengeance: he killed Nithhad's sons and raped his daughter, Beadohild. This outrage is seen from the point of view of the victim, who is terrified at her pregnancy. Her consolation, known to the audience but unsaid, is that her child, Widia, became a great hero. The third strophe refers more obscurely to a similar act of rape, for which some compensating reversal of fortune must have been known. The fourth strophe tells of the rule of Theodoric of Merano, which lasted long but came to an end; the fifth of the tyranny of Eormanric the Goth, which also came to an end.

After a passage on how Providence can bring joy out of sorrow, in the final strophe the poet reveals that he is Deor, and tells his own misfortune: long the court poet of the Heodenings, he has been cast aside in favour of a rival poet. On a Boethian version of the principle that worse things have happened at sea, the refrain of *Deor* expresses the hope that the injustice done to the poet may be rectified or endured, as greater wrongs have been.

Deor

Wayland knew the wanderer's fate:
that single-willed earl suffered agonies,
sorrow and longing the sole companions
of his ice-cold exile. Anxieties bit
when Nithhad put a knife to his hamstrings,
laid clever bonds on the better man.

That went by; this may too.

Beadohild mourned her murdered brothers:
but her own plight pained her more
– her womb grew great with child.
When she knew that, she could never hold
steady before her wit what was to happen.

That went by; this may too.

All have heard of Hild's ravishing:
the Geat's lust was ungovernable,
their bitter love banished sleep.

That went by; this may too.

Thirty winters Theodoric ruled
the Maering city: and many knew it.

That went by; this may too.

We all know that Eormanric
had a wolf's wit. Wide Gothland
lay in the grasp of that grim king,
and through it many sat, by sorrows environed,
foreseeing only sorrow; sighed for the downfall
and thorough overthrow of the thrall-maker.

That went by; this may too.

When each gladness has gone, gathering sorrow
may cloud the brain; and in his breast a man
cannot then see how his sorrows shall end.

But he may think how throughout this world
it is the way of God, who is wise, to deal
to the most part of men much favour
and a flourishing fame; to a few the sorrow-share.

Of myself in this regard I shall say this only:
that in the hall of the Heodenings I held long the
          makarship,
lived dear to my prince, Deor my name;
many winters I held this happy place
and my lord was kind. Then came Heorrenda,
whose lays were skilful; the lord of fighting-men
settled on him the estate bestowed once on me.

          That went by; this may too.

PASSAGES FROM *BEOWULF*

This poem is found in the manuscript known as Cotton Vitellius A.xv. Now kept in the British Library, it was once the fifteenth volume on shelf A in a bookcase below a bust of the Roman emperor Vitellius, one of a series of bookcases crowned with imperial busts in the library of Sir Robert Cotton at Ashburnham House, London. Posterity has paused on the name of this house, for many of the manuscripts in its library were burned to ash in a fire in 1731; though not on the name Vitellius, which means 'Calf'.

Vitellius A.xv was charred at the edges and marginal characters were lost. Others have disappeared since then, as can be seen from two transcripts of the poem about Beowulf which were made later in that century, when Cotton Vitellius A.xv was in the British Museum. The poem was first edited by the man who made one of the transcripts and commissioned the other: G. J. Thorkelin, a servant of the Danish crown. He published it in Copenhagen in 1815 under a title which described it as a poem about Danish history in the Anglo-Saxon dialect. (The word 'dialect' was a reminder that the Danish king Canute had been King of England from 1015 to 1035.) Thorkelin also provided a Latin translation. The poem was first called *Beowulf* in the first English edition, 1833, made by John M. Kemble. A considerable number of learned editions of this damaged text have since been published in several countries, especially in Germany, the UK and the USA, and the text now includes over a thousand editorial emendations. *Beowulf* has been translated hundreds of times into modern languages, first into Danish by the poet N. F. S. Grundtvig in 1820, and then into the languages of Europe and other countries. There are seven versions in Japanese. It has long been recognized as the best poem in Old English, and has attracted literary scholars such as W. P. Ker, and poet-translators from Grundtvig and Tennyson to Longfellow and William Morris and so on down to Edwin Morgan, myself and Seamus Heaney. The blind Argentinian writer Jorge Luis Borges, when he came to St

Andrews, asked to be taken to the edge of the North Sea so
that he could recite *Beowulf* at it from memory. The story has
been made into several films, and into a Brazilian comic book
called *O mostro di Caim*. (Grendel, the monster killed by
Beowulf, descends from Cain.) *Beowulf* has become strangely
popular.

But at the time when I began on *The Earliest English Poems*,
I found *Beowulf* daunting. This was not an uncommon reaction
among undergraduates obliged to climb the sacred mountain
of early English literature under the gaze of philologists. The
poem was impressive, but dense, difficult, strange and remote.
To understand it properly cost so much work! And the idea
that all students of *Beowulf* might aspire to be textual editors
could deter the easily deterred. Penguin Classics asked me to
translate it, but I declined. I accepted a later invitation, pub-
lishing a verse translation in 1973, followed in 1995 by an
edition of the text, also in Penguin Classics, in which each page
is faced by a page on which nearly every word is glossed. But
in 1960 I found the shorter poems easier to deal with and in
need of retranslation. *Beowulf*, nevertheless, had grand pass-
ages which made sense on their own. I translated four of these,
adding a fifth in a later edition.

Those who want to read the epic are referred to the editions
and translations given in Further Reading. *Beowulf*, to be brief,
is a condensed epic poem set in southern Scandinavia among
the heathen ancestors of the dynasties who, at the time of
the poem's composition, ruled in a Christian England. Each
translated passage is prefaced by an indication of where it
comes in the narrative.

The Funeral of Scyld Shefing

The first half of the poem is set at the court of Hrothgar (Roger),
a king of the Scylding dynasty which ruled in sixth-century
Denmark. Scyld, the founder of this family, had arrived by
water as a child, rather like Moses in the bulrushes, but lived
to create an empire. Here his body is placed in a ship which is
taken out to sea. Burial ships have been found buried in mounds

on the foreshores of Sweden, and one was found at Sutton Hoo in Suffolk, in 1939, on the eve of war with Germany. This oak-built ship, 29 metres in length, contained princely grave goods with much gold, silver and magnificent armour. It had been dragged up the shore and buried under a mound. Coins in a purse help to date the burial: it is usually identified as the grave of Raedwald, the powerful ruler of the East Angles, who died in 632. Bede presents Raedwald as a convert who relapsed and compromised with the old gods. The Sutton Hoo burial is essentially pagan, furnishing the buried man with food and drink and all the credentials of earthly rank and power which he would need to establish his importance in heathen Valhalla, the feasting-hall of the great dead. Yet the grave goods also contain baptismal spoons and a nest of cross-incised silver bowls from Constantinople.

The poem raises the question of the ultimate destination of Scyld and his treasure, leaving it enigmatic but ominous: 'men did not know who unloaded that cargo'. This recalls Bede's story of the counsellor of King Edwin of Northumbria who likened the life of man to a sparrow that flies in through the lighted hall where the king and his friends are feasting and flies out again into the dark. The king and his counsellors accept Christian teachings about the afterlife as superior to pagan ignorance.

Beowulf (lines 26–52)

At the hour shaped for him Scyld departed,
the many-strengthed moved into his Master's keeping.

They carried him out to the current sea,
his sworn arms-fellows, as he himself had asked
while he wielded by his words, Warden of the Scyldings,
beloved folk-founder; long had he ruled.

A boat with a ringed neck rode in the haven,
icy, out-eager, the atheling's vessel,
and there they laid out their lord and master,

dealer of wound gold, in the waist of the ship,
in majesty by the mast.
                              A mound of treasures
from far countries was fetched aboard her,
and it is said that no boat was ever more bravely fitted
     out
with the weapons of a warrior, war accoutrement,
bills and byrnies; on his breast were set
treasures and trappings to travel with him
on his far faring into the flood's sway.

This hoard was not less great than the gifts he had
from those who sent him, on the sill of life,
over seas, alone, a small child.

High over head they hoisted and fixed
a gold *signum*; gave him to the flood,
let the seas take him, with sour hearts
and mourning moods. Men have not the knowledge
to say with any truth – however tall beneath the heavens,
however much listened to – who unloaded that boat.

Beowulf's Voyage to Denmark

Hrothgar, King of Denmark, prospers and builds a great hall,
Heorot (Hart, Stag), which archaeologists can now confidently
locate at Lejre, near Roskilde, west of Copenhagen. He rules
a wide empire, latterly with the support of his nephew,
Hrothwulf. Heorot is then attacked at night by an envious
fiend, later named Grendel: demon, man, monster and of the
kindred of Cain. Grendel enters Heorot by night and devours
the bodies of Hrothgar's retainers. Repeating these nightly
raids, Grendel terrorizes Heorot for twelve years.

Beowulf hears of this in Geatland, in what is now southern
Sweden, ruled by his mother's brother, Hygelac, King of the
Geats. The sun shines on Beowulf's ship as it sails from Geat-
land to Denmark, where he is met by a courteous challenge
from a noble warrior who guards the coast. It is a bright and
Homeric passage.

Beowulf (lines 194–257)

Grendel was known of then in Geatland across the sea
to one of Hygelac's followers, the first of his thanes
and for main strength of all men first
that trod ground at the time being;
build and blood matched.

                      He bade a seaworthy
wave-cutter be fitted out for him; the warrior king
he would seek, he said, over swan's riding,
that lord of name, needing men.

The wiser sought to dissuade him from voyaging
hardly or not at all, though they held him dear;
whetted his quest-thirst, watched omens.

The prince had already picked his men
from the folk's flower, the fiercest among them
that might be found. With fourteen men,
sought sound-wood: sea-wise Beowulf
led them right down to the land's edge.

Time running on, she rode the waves now
hard in by headland. Harnessed warriors
stepped on her stem; setting tide churned
sea with sand, soldiers carried
bright mail-coats to the mast's foot,
war-gear well wrought; willingly they shoved her out,
thorough-braced craft, on the craved voyage.

Away she went over a wavy ocean,
boat like a bird, breaking seas,
wind-whetted, white-throated,
till curved prow had ploughed so far
– the sun standing right on the second day –
that they might see land loom on the skyline,
then the shimmer of cliffs, sheer moors behind,
reaching capes.
                The crossing was at an end;

closed the wake. Weather-Geats
stood on strand, stepped briskly up;
a rope going ashore, ring-mail clashed,
battle-girdings. God they thanked
for the smooth going over the salt-trails.
The watchman saw them. From the wall where he stood,
posted by the Scyldings to patrol the cliffs,
he saw the polished lindens pass along the gangway
and the clean equipment. Curiosity
moved him to know who these men might be.

Hrothgar's thane, when his horse had picked
its way down to the shore, shook his spear
fiercely at arm's length, framed the challenge:
'Strangers, you have steered this steep craft
through the sea-ways, sought our coast.
I see you are warriors; you wear that dress now.
I must ask who you are. In all the years
I have lived as look-out at land's end here
– so that no foreigners with a fleet-army
might land in Denmark and do us harm –
shield-carriers have never come ashore
more openly. You had no assurance
of welcome here, word of leave
from Hrothgar and Hrothwulf!
                              I have not in my life
set eyes on a man with more might in his frame
than this helmed lord. That's no hall-fellow
worthied with weapons; or well counterfeited,
for he has a hero's look.
                          I must have your names now
and the names of your fathers; or further you shall not go
as undeclared spies into the Danish land.

Stay where you are, strangers, hear
what I have to say! Seas crossed,
it is best and simplest straightaway to acknowledge
where you are from, why you have come.'

To Grendelsmere and Back

Grendel has come to Heorot at night. He is delighted to find men sleeping there once more: Beowulf and his Geats. He grabs and consumes one man and reaches out for a second, who is Beowulf himself. Grendel can end the ensuing hand-to-hand struggle only by tearing himself away, leaving his arm behind him; he makes his way back to his home in a mere up on the moors. Our passage begins here. This passage has an additional value for its picture of the impromptu composition of poetry on horseback. At its end, Beowulf is compared with Sigemund, the greatest of dragon-slayers.

Beowulf (lines 837–75)

There was, as I heard it, at hall next morning
a great gathering in gift-hall yard
to see the wonder. Along wide highroads
the clanchiefs came from close and far away
onto the killer's trail; and with truth it may be said
that there was not among them one man sorry
to see the spoor-blood of that blind rush
for the monster's mere, when his mood had sickened
with every step-stagger, strength broken,
dragging deathwards his dribbling life.

The tarn was troubled; a terrible wave-thrash
brimmed it, bubbling; black-mingled,
the warm wound-blood welled upwards.
Here the death-marked dived, here died with no gladness;
in the fen-moor lair he laid aside
his heathen soul. Hell welcomed it.

Then the older retainers turned back on the way
journeyed so joyfully; joined by the young men,
warriors on white horses wheeled away from the mere
in bold mood. Beowulf's feat
was much spoken of, and many said

that between the seas, south or north,
over earth's stretch no other man
beneath sky's shifting excelled Beowulf,
of all sword-wielders worthiest of empire.
In saying this they did not slight in the least
the gracious Hrothgar, for he was a good king.

Where as they went their way broadened
they would match their mounts, making them leap
along the best stretches, the strife-eager
on their fallow horses.
                Or a fellow of the king's
whose head was a storehouse of the storied verse,
whose tongue gave gold to the language
of the treasured repertory, wrought a new lay
made in the measure.
                The man struck up,
found the phrase, framed rightly
the deed of Beowulf, drove the tale,
rang word-changes. He chose to speak
first of Sigemund, sang the most part
of what he had heard of that hero's exploits. . . .

The Lament of the Last Survivor

Grendel is avenged by a second monster, his mere-dwelling
mother, who kills Hrothgar's favourite retainer at Heorot.
Beowulf is taken to the mere, where he dives in, kills Grendel's
mother, and brings back the head of Grendel to Heorot. He
returns to Geatland, and, after the deaths of Hygelac and his
son, accedes to the throne. He has ruled Geatland well for fifty
years when his hall is burned down by a dragon, in vengeance
for a thief having taken a golden cup from the underground
hoard which it guards.

    This is the point at which the poet imagines how the golden
hoard came to be in the underground chamber. The speech
of the imagined Last Survivor, the lament for the heroes that
are gone, has parallels in *The Ruin*, *The Wanderer* and *The*

Seafarer, but here the note is one of sorrow and regret unqualified by any other perspective.

Beowulf (lines 2231–66)

There were heaps of hoard-things in this hall underground
which once in gone days gleamed and rang;
the treasure of a race rusting derelict.

In another age an unknown man,
brows bent, brought and hid here
the beloved hoard. The whole race
death-rapt, and of the ring of earls
one left alive; living on in that place
heavy with friend-loss, the hoard-guard
waited the same wierd. His wit acknowledged
that the treasures gathered and guarded over the years
were his for the briefest while.
                              Barrow stood ready
on flat ground where breakers beat at the headland,
new, near at hand, made narrow of access.
The keeper of rings carried into it
the earls' holdings, the hoard-worthy part
fraught with gold, few words spoke:
'Hold, ground, the gold of the earls!
Men could not. Cowards they were not
who took it from thee once, but war-death took them,
that stops life, struck them, spared not one
man of my people, passed on now.
They have had their hall-joys. I have not with me
a man able to unsheathe this. . . .
Who shall polish this plated vessel?
This cup was dear. The company is elsewhere.

This hardened helmet healed with gold
shall lose its shell. They sleep now
whose work was to burnish the battle-mask;
so the cuirass that in the crash took

bite of iron amid breaking shields:
it moulders with the man. This mailshirt travelled far,
hung from a shoulder shouldered warriors;
it shall not jingle again.
                              There's no joy from harp-play,
gleewood's gladness, no good hawk
swings through hall now, no swift horse
tramps at threshold. The threat came:
falling has felled a flowering kingdom.'

Beowulf's Funeral

Beowulf has killed the dragon but is fatally wounded. Without
his protection, the people of the Geats now foresee that they
will be conquered by the Swedes, a fear which makes more
sombre still their elaborate and magnificent farewell to the last
of the heroes. Arms and armour are burned with the body, a
woman mourns for Beowulf and utters forebodings, and the
retainers build for him a barrow on the headland, as he had
requested. The twelve men who ride round the barrow pro-
nounce his epitaph in the poem's final words. This too is a
Homeric passage, but it dwells more on Beowulf's care for his
people than on his desire for glory.

Beowulf (lines 3137–82)

The Geat race then reared up for him
a funeral pyre. It was not a petty mound,
but shining mail-coats and shields of war
and helmets hung upon it, as he had desired.
Then the heroes, lamenting, laid out in the middle
their great chief, their cherished lord.
On top of the mound the men then kindled
the biggest of funeral-fires. Black wood-smoke
arose from the blaze, and the roaring of flames
mingled with weeping. The winds lay still
as the heat at the fire's heart consumed

the house of bone. And in heavy mood
they uttered their sorrow at the slaughter of their lord.

A woman of the Geats in grief sang out
the lament for his death. Loudly she sang,
her hair bound up, the burden of her fear
that evil days were destined her
– troops cut down, terror of armies,
bondage, humiliation. Heaven swallowed the smoke.

Then the Storm-Geat nation constructed for him
a stronghold on the headland, so high and broad
that seafarers might see it from afar.
The beacon to that battle-reckless man
they made in ten days. What remained from the fire
they cast a wall around, of workmanship
as fine as their wisest men could frame for it.
They placed in the tomb both the torques and the jewels,
all the magnificence that the men had earlier
taken from the hoard in hostile mood.
They left the earls' wealth in the earth's keeping,
the gold in the dirt. It dwells there yet,
of no more use to men than in ages before.

Then the warriors rode around the barrow,
twelve of them in all, athelings' sons.
They recited a dirge to declare their grief,
spoke of the man, mourned their king.
They praised his manhood and the prowess of his hands,
they raised his name; it is right a man
should be lavish in honouring his lord and friend,
should love him in his heart when the leading-forth
from the house of flesh befalls him at last.

This was the manner of the mourning of the men of the
        Geats,
sharers in the feast, at the fall of their lord:
they said that he was of all the world's kings
the gentlest of men, and the most gracious,
the kindest to his people, the keenest for fame.

THE FIGHT AT FINNSBURGH

This fragment of text, also known as *Finnsburh* and *The Finnsburh Fragment*, survives, like *The Battle of Maldon*, in a transcript made early in the eighteenth century by an anti-quarian, George Hickes, in his *Linguarum Veterum Septentrionalium Thesaurus Grammatico-Criticus et Archaeologicus* (*Treasury of the Ancient Northern Languages*), published in Oxford in 1705. According to Hickes, the text was found on a single leaf in a manuscript of homilies written in 'semi-Saxon' in Lambeth Palace, London. The leaf was subsequently lost.

The background to this incident is rapidly and allusively recounted in the Finn episode in *Beowulf*, an embedded narrative, one purpose of which is to act as an example of how marriages arranged between the children of feuding peoples fail to bring lasting peace. The *Fragment*, by contrast, is a simple poem of action with none of the reflectiveness or complexity of *Beowulf*. In a classic situation, Hnaef and his men are treacherously attacked by their hosts. Hnaef, a Dane, had been paying a visit to his half-sister Hildeburgh, at the hall of her husband, Finn, leader of the Frisians. The *Fragment* recounts a night attack on the guest hall allocated to the Danish visitors. The narration is dramatic, yet contains elements found in other fights in heroic literature: comradeship, sacrifice, brave words, actions and deaths, the birds and beasts who gather to feast upon the slain, the sustained defence of a narrow place, the interplay of weapons, the display of known names. Today the only name we recognize is Hengest, a Jute on Hnaef's side, a key figure in the fuller version of the story relayed in *Beowulf*. He may also be the same man as the Hengest who led the Jutes invited to Kent in 449, but of this we cannot be certain.

The Fight at Finnsburgh

'. . . the horns of the house, hall-gables burning?'

Battle-young Hnaef broke silence:
'It is not the eaves aflame, nor in the east yet
does day break; no dragon flies this way.
It is the soft clashing of claymores you hear
that they carry to the house.
       Soon shall be the cough of birds,
hoar wolf's howl, hard wood-talk,
shield's answer to shaft.
       Now shines the moon,
welkin-wanderer. The woes at hand
shall bring to the full this folk's hatred for us.

Awake! on your feet! Who fights for me?
Hold your lindens right, hitch up your courage,
think bravely, be with me at the doors!'

The gold-clad thanes rose, girt on their swords.
Two doubtless soldiers stepped to the door,
Sigeferth and Eaha, with their swords out,
and Ordlaf and Guthlaf to the other door went,
Hengest himself hastening in their steps.

Hearing these adversaries advance on the door
Guthere held on to Garulf so he should not
front the rush to force the threshold
and risk his life, whose loss could not be remedied;
but clear above their whispers he called out his demand
– brave heart – Who held the door?

'My name is Sigeferth, of the Secgan, chief,
known through the seas. I have seen a few battles
and known troubles. What you intend for me
your own flesh shall be the first to taste.'

Then swung strokes sounded along the wall;
wielded by the brave, the bone-shielding

boss-boards split. Burg-floor spoke,
and Garulf fell at last in the fighting at the door,
Garulf, the first man in the Frisian islands,
son to Guthlaf, and good men lay round,
a pale crowd of corpses. The crows dangled
black and brown. Blades clashing
flashed fire – as though all Finnsburgh were ablaze.

Never have sixty swordmen in a set fight
borne themselves more bravely; or better I have not
    heard of.
Never was the bright mead better earned
than that which Hnaef gave his guard of youth.

They fought and none fell. On the fifth day
the band was still whole and still held the doors.
Then a wounded warrior went to the side,
said his ring-coat was riven to pieces,
stout hauberk though it was, and that his helm had gone
    through.
The folk's shepherd and shielder asked him
how the braves bore their wounds
and which of the young men. . . .

THE BATTLE OF BRUNANBURGH

This poem, also known as *Brunanburgh* or *Brunanburh*, forms the entire entry for the year 937 in four of the seven manuscripts of the *Anglo-Saxon Chronicle*. It celebrates a great victory won by Wessex over its enemies, and is the first poem to appear in the *Chronicle*. King Athelstan and his brother Edmund, the grandsons of Alfred, defeated, with the help of the Mercians, a large invading force. The invaders were led by Constantine III, King of Scots, whose force also included Picts; by Owen, King of the British of Strathclyde; and by Anlaf. This was the formidable Olaf Guthfrithson, King of the Dublin Vikings, who had been joined by those Norsemen whom King Athelstan had previously driven out of Northumbria. Brunanburgh was a major battle ensuring the future of the Wessex dynasty as rulers of a united England. The place itself may be in the north Midlands or the north-west of England, possibly Bromburgh, Cheshire, on the Wirral shore of the Mersey. The poem is rather in the style of Handel's *Zadok the Priest* and gives few details of the battle, especially compared with *The Battle of Maldon*. But foreign annals confirm the casualties at the battle and its importance.

By this stage, the Saxons had been settled in England for more than four centuries, and the traditional heroic verse had had to adapt to changes in the language, in literacy and in patronage. *Brunanburgh* is the first royal praise-poem, the first court poem, the first heroic poem in a chronicle, the first poem to mention the reading of historical books, and the last to observe the correct versification. It is like a tattered regimental banner, deploying superbly all the proud old figures: the brothers were worthy of their ancestry, they broke through the board-wall of overlapping shields, the fallen were many and noble, the beasts of battle feasted well. It is difficult to translate this without cliché, though Tennyson managed to do so in his own musical style. Indeed, *Brunanburgh* is a difficult poem to translate at all, for in translation the distinction with which the old formulas are used is not easy to convey, though this is ideally more possible in verse than in prose.

The poet understood his business, as is shown in the long periphrasis for the length of this day of slaughter in lines 12–17. It makes telling use also of the tradition of understatement, as when the death of Constantine's son is introduced after the long sentence which begins 'He had no need to rejoice'.

The Battle of Brunanburgh

Athelstan the King, captain of men,
ring-giver of warriors – and with him his brother
Edmund the Atheling – unending glory
won in that strife by their swords' edges
that there was about Brunanburgh.
               The board-wall they cut through,
cleft the lindens with the leavings of hammers,
Edward's offspring, answering the blood
they had from their forebears:
               that in the field they should often
against every foe defend the land,
hoard and homes. The hated ones fell,
the people of the Scots and the shipmen too,
fell as was fated. The field was running
with the blood of soldiers from the sun's rise
at the hour of the morning when that marvellous star,
God's bright candle, glided over the lands,
to the time when the creature of the eternal Lord
sank to rest. Then sated with battle
and weary lay many there, men of the Northerners
shot above their shields, and Scotsmen likewise,
wasted by spears.
               The West Saxons
rode in troop right through the day
hard on the heels of the hated peoples,
pursuing hewed fiercely at the fleeing warriors
with mill-sharpened swords. The Mercians did not refuse
the hard hand-play to any hero among those
who with Anlaf over the ocean's courses
in the bosom of a ship had sought our land
and their doom in that fight.
               There were five kings
who in their youth lay low on that battlefield,
slain by the sword; and seven earls
of Anlaf's also; others without number

of shipmen and Scots. With scant retinue
the Prince of the Northmen was put to flight
by stark need to the stern of his craft:
the long ship drove out across the dark waters;
the King slipped away, saved his life.

The Old King likewise came away also,
the grey-haired campaigner, Constantine, fled
to the North he knew. He had no need to rejoice
in that meeting of swords where he was shortened of
     kinsmen
and deprived of friends on the field of assembly,
plucked on the battlefield: on that place of slaughter
he left his son brought low by wounds,
young on the battlefield. The yield of the swords
gave no ground for boasting to the grey-haired chieftain,
the old enemy; to Anlaf neither.

They had no cause to laugh with those left from the war,
that they had been the better in battle-accomplishment
on the field of strife when the standards clashed,
at the spear-meeting when men came together
in the exchange of weapons: when with Edward's sons
they had played together in the place of slaughter.
     The nailed ships of the Norsemen took off
what spears had spared, a spattered remnant,
across deep Dingsmere to Dublin once more,
to seek again Ireland in shame.
The brothers also, both of them together,
the King and the Atheling, came away to their own,
the West-Saxon land, in war-triumph.
The corpse-sharers, shadowy-coated,
they left behind them: the black raven
with its horny beak; the brown eagle
of white tail-feather, to feast on the slain
– greedy war-hawk; and the grey one,
the wolf of the weald.
                    No worse slaughter

in this island has ever yet
before these days befallen a people
by the edge of the sword – so say the books,
the wise men of old – since from the East came
Angles and Saxons up to these shores,
seeking Britain across the broad seas,
smart for glory, those smiths of war
that overcame the Welsh, and won a homeland.

THE BATTLE OF MALDON

If Brunanburgh in 937 was a major victory in pitched battle for the rulers of England over invaders from the north, Maldon in 991 was a defeat for the East Anglian militia at the hands of a larger Viking force. But the poem on the defeat at Maldon is a vivid, detailed and coherent account of the battle, from which, with the help of the *Anglo-Saxon Chronicle*, the action can be reconstructed and located on a map. The Viking host sailed up from Ipswich and beached their long ships on an island in the tidal estuary of the River Blackwater (then called the Pant). Northey, as this island is now called, is linked to the southern shore by a causeway ('the bridge'), covered twice a day by the tide. *The Battle of Maldon*, also known as *Maldon*, is a satisfying and moving recital, and may be the best battle poem in English.

The entry in the Parker version of the *Chronicle* reads '993 [for 991]: In this year came Anlaf with 93 ships to Folkestone, and harried outside, and sailed thence to Sandwich, and thence

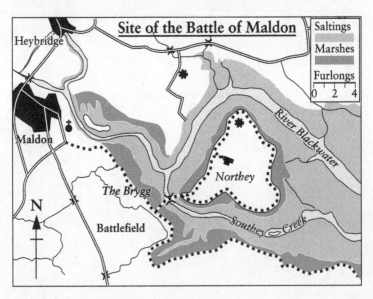

to Ipswich, overrunning all the countryside, and so on to Maldon. Ealdorman Byrhtnoth [spelt 'Bryhtnoth' in the translation for reasons of euphony] came to meet them with his levies and fought them, but they slew the ealdorman there [10 August] and had possession of the place of slaughter.' The Laud version of the *Chronicle* records that 'it was decided in this year for the first time to pay tribute to the Danes'. The ten thousand pounds paid was the first instalment of Danegeld, the payment of gold to Danes to make them go away. Undeterred, they came back to Aethelred's England, and back again, and twenty-four years after this battle became rulers of England.

The poem survives only in the transcript made shortly before the fire at Sir Robert Cotton's library referred to on p. 73. It lacks a beginning and an end, but perhaps not many lines are lost. The text opens with two symbolic actions: the Ealdorman (the Earl of the translation) sends away the horses; the young man sends away his hawk. No retreat from the invaders; no time for sport. In what follows there are typical scenes: Byrhtnoth riding up and down arranging the positions of his troops, the defence of the causeway, the exchange of speeches demanding tribute and offering defiance, the beasts and birds of battle. The later stages of the battle are recounted in a series of type-scenes: speech, advance, death, general encounter, speech, advance, death. There are standard speeches of courage and loyalty, pride in ancestry, patriotism and piety. These were not the exact words used on the field, nor might soldiers have had leisure to listen to such words, though combat will have had its rules. Yet, however formalized and idealized, the poem carries conviction. This may be a literary rather than an historical judgement, but that does not make it incorrect.

The poem shows the defeat as the result of a strategic mistake, an act of cowardice, and a second mistake. The first mistake (according to some) was Byrhtnoth's allowing the Vikings to cross the causeway, for they would otherwise have had to sail their ninety-three ships away somewhere else. But Byrhtnoth clearly held that the raiders must be resisted at any cost, and would certainly not see his own death, or even the defeat, as invalidating this judgement. After the death of the Earl, a

coward rides away on the only horse – Byrhtnoth's horse.
Many who followed the rider believed that the deserter was
Byrhtnoth, says the poet; who represents the personal body-
guard of the Earl as fighting on to the death. The last speech in
the text we have gives classic expression to the heroic code.
Byrhtnoth himself is well documented, and the names of the
poem are in local charters. *Maldon* is specifically rooted in its
area, and represents local memories. It may well have been
composed as a memorial at the nearby Abbey of Ramsey, which
Byrhtnoth had endowed. He was a local hero.

The Battle of Maldon

... would be broken.

Then he bade each man let go bridles,
drive far the horses and fare forward,
fit thought to hand-work and heart to fighting.

Whereat one of Offa's kin, knowing the Earl
would not suffer slack-heartedness,
loosed from his wrist his loved hawk;
over the wood it stooped: he stepped to battle.
By that a man might know this young man's will
to weaken not at the war-play: he had taken up weapons.

Eadric also would serve the Earl,
his lord, in the fight. He went forth
with spear to battle, his spirit failed not
while he with hand might yet hold
board and broadsword: he made good his boast
to stand fast in fight before his lord.

Then Bryhtnoth dressed his band of warriors,
from horseback taught each man his task,
where he should stand, how keep his station.
He bade them brace their linden-boards aright,
fast in finger-grip, and to fear not.
Then when his folk was fairly ranked,
Bryhtnoth alighted where he loved best to be
and was held most at heart – among hearth-companions.

Then stood on strand and called out sternly
a Viking spokesman. He made speech –
threat in his throat, threw across the seamen's
errand to the Earl where he stood on our shore.

   'The swift-striking seafarers send me to thee,
   bid me say that thou send for thy safety
   rings, bracelets. Better for you
   that you stay straightaway our onslaught with tribute

than that we should share bitter strife.
We need not meet if you can meet our needs:
for a gold tribute a truce is struck.

Art captain here: if thou tak'st this course,
art willing to pay thy people's ransom,
wilt render to Vikings what they think right,
buying our peace at our price,
we shall with that tribute turn back to ship,
fare out on the flood, and hold you as friends.'

Bryhtnoth spoke. He raised shield-board,
shook the slim ash-spear, shaped his words.
Stiff with anger, he gave him answer:

'Hearest 'ou, seaman, what this folk sayeth?
Spears shall be all the tribute they send you,
viper-stained spears and the swords of forebears,
such a haul of harness as shall hardly profit you.

Spokesman for scavengers, go speak this back again,
bear your tribe a bitterer tale:
that there stands here 'mid his men not the meanest of
        Earls,
pledged to fight in this land's defence,
the land of Aethelred, my liege lord,
its soil, its folk. In this fight the heathen
shall fall. It would be a shame for your trouble
if you should with our silver away to ship
without fight offered. It is a fair step hither:
you have come a long way into our land.

But English silver is not so softly won:
first iron and edge shall make arbitrament,
harsh war-trial, ere we yield tribute.'

He bade his brave men bear their shields forward
until they all stood at the stream's edge,
though they might not clash yet for the cleaving waters.
After the ebb the flood came flowing in;
the sea's arms locked. Overlong it seemed

before they might bear spear-shafts in shock together.
So they stood by Panta's stream in proud array,
the ranks of the East Saxons and the host from the ash-ships,
nor might any of them harm another
save who through arrow-flight fell dead.

The flood went out. Eager the fleet-men stood,
the crowding raiders, ravening for battle;
then the heroes' Helm bade hold the causeway
a war-hard warrior – Wulfstan was his name –
come of brave kin. It was this Ceola's son
who with his Frankish spear struck down the first man there
as he so boldly stepped onto the bridge's stonework.

There stood with Wulfstan staunch warriors,
Aelfere and Maccus, men of spirit
who would not take flight from the ford's neck
but fast defence make against the foemen
the while that they might wield their weapons.
When the hated strangers saw and understood
what bitter bridge-warders were brought against them there,
they began to plead with craft, craving leave
to fare over the ford and lead across their footmen.

Then the Earl was overswayed by his heart's arrogance
to allow overmuch land to that loath nation:
the men stood silent as Brighthelm's son
called out over the cold water.

> 'The ground is cleared for you: come quickly to us,
> gather to battle. God alone knows
> who shall carry the wielding of this waste ground.'

The war-wolves waded across, mourned not for the water,
the Viking warrior-band; came west over Pant,
bearing shield-boards over sheer water
and up onto land, lindenwood braced.

Against their wrath there stood in readiness
Bryhtnoth amid his band. He bade them work

the war-hedge with their targes, and the troop to stand
fast against foe. Then neared the fight,
the glory-trial. The time grew on
when there the fated men must fall;
the war-cry was raised up. Ravens wound higher,
the eagle, carrion-eager; on earth – the cry!

Out flashed file-hard point from fist,
sharp-ground spears sprang forth,
bows were busy, bucklers flinched,
it was a bitter battle-clash. On both halves
brave men fell, boys lay still.

It was then that Wulfmaer was wounded, war-rest chose,
Bryhtnoth's kinsman; he was beaten down,
his sister's son, under the swords' flailing.
But straight wreaking requital on the Vikings,
Edward (as I heard) so struck one man
– the sword-arm stiff, not stinting the blow –
that the fated warrior fell at his feet:
deed for which Bryhtnoth, when a breathing space came,
spoke his thanks to his bower-thane.

So they stood fast, those stout-hearted
warriors at the war-play, watching fiercely
who there with spear might first dispatch
a doomed man's life. The dying fell to earth;
others stood steadfast. Bryhtnoth stirred them,
bade every man there turn mood to deeds
who would that day's doom wrest from out the Danish ranks.

Bryhtnoth war-hard braced shield-board,
shook out his sword, strode firmly
towards his enemy, earl to churl,
in either's heart harm to the other.

The sea-man sped his southern spear
so that it wounded the warriors' lord
who with his shield checked, so that the shaft burst,

shivered the spear-head; it sprang away.
Stung then to anger he stabbed with ash-point
the proud sea-warrior that wrought him his wound,
old in war-skills let the weapon drive
through the man's throat, his thrust steered
so as to reach right to the reaver's life-breath.
And afresh he struck him, stabbed so swiftly
that the ring-braid burst apart; breast pierced
through the locked hauberk, in his heart stood
the embittered ash-point. The Earl was the blither,
his brave mood laughed, loud thanks he made
for the day's work the Lord had dealt him.

Flashed a dart from Danish hand,
fist-driven, and flew too truly,
bit the Earl, Aethelred's thane.
There stood at his side a stripling warrior,
young Wulfmaer, Wulfstan's son,
fresh to the field. In a flash he
plucked from its place the blood-black point,
flung back the filed spear; again it flew.
Home sank the steel, stretched on the plain
him who so late had pierced the Prince so grievously.

A mailed man then moved towards the Earl
thinking to strip him of his steel harness,
war-dress, armbands and ornate sword.
Bryhtnoth broke out brand from sheath,
broad, bright-bladed, and on the breastplate struck,
but one of the spoilers cut short the blow,
his swing unstringing the Earl's sword-arm.

He yielded to the ground the yellow-hilted sword,
strengthless to hold the hard blade longer up
or wield weapon. One word more,
the hoar-headed warrior, heartening his men:
he bade them go forward, good companions.
Fast on his feet he might not further stand.

He looked to heaven. . . .

> 'I give Thee thanks, Lord God of hosts,
> for I have known in this world a wealth of gladness,
> but now, mild Maker, I have most need
> that Thou grant my ghost grace for this journey
> so that my soul may unscathed cross
> into Thy keeping, King of angels,
> pass through in peace: my prayer is this,
> that the hates of hell may not harm her.'

Then they hewed him down, the heathen churls,
and with him those warriors, Wulfmaer and Aelfnoth,
who had stood at his side: stretched on the field,
the two followers fellowed in death.

Then did the lack-willed leave the battlefield;
Odda's kin came first away:
Godric turned, betrayed the lord
who had made him a gift of many good horses.
He leaped onto the harness that had been Bryhtnoth's,
unrightfully rode in his place,
and with him his brothers both ran,
Godwine and Godwiy, who had no gust for fighting;
they wheeled from the war to the wood's fastness,
sought shelter and saved their lives;
and more went with them than were at all meet
had they called to mind the many heart-claims
Bryhtnoth had wrought them, worthying them.

This Offa had told him on an earlier day
at the council-place when he had called a meeting,
that many gathered there who were making brave
        speeches
would not hold in the hour of need.
And now the folk's father had fallen lifeless,
Aethelred's Earl. All the hearthsharers
might see their lord lying dead.

Proudly the thanes pressed forward,

uncowed the warriors crowded eager
for one of two things: each man wanted
either to requite that death or to quit life.
Aelfric's son sped them on,
a warrior young in winters; his words rang
keen in the air. Aelfwine called out:

> 'Remember the speeches spoken over mead,
> battle-vows on the bench, the boasts we vaunted,
> heroes in hall, against the harsh war-trial!
> *Now* shall be proven the prowess of the man.
>
> I would that you all hear my high descendance:
> know that in Mercia I am of mighty kin,
> that my grandfather was the great Ealhelm,
> wise Earl, world-blessed man.
> Shall the princes of that people reproach Aelfwine
> that he broke from the banded bulwark of the Angles
> to seek his own land, with his lord lying
> felled on the field? Fiercest of griefs!
> Beside that he was my lord he was allied to me in
>   blood.'

Then he advanced on the Vikings intent on vengeance.
Straight his spearpoint sprang at a man
among the press of pirates, pitched him to the ground,
killed outright. Then he called to his companions,
friends and fellow-thanes to come forth to battle.

Offa spoke, shook his ash-spear:

> 'In right good time dost thou recall us to
> our allegiance, Aelfwine. Now that the Earl who led us
> lies on the earth, we all need
> each and every thane to urge forth the other
> warriors to the war while weapon lives
> quick in a hand, hardened blade,
> spear or good sword. Godric the coward,
> the coward son of Odda, has undone us all:
> too many in our ranks, when he rode away

on Bryhtnoth's big horse, believed it was the Earl,
and we are scattered over the field. The folk is split,
shield-wall shattered. Shame on that defection
that has betrayed into retreat the better half of the
    army!'

Linden-board high-lifted, Leofsunu stood;
from the shadow of his shield shouted out this answer:

'I swear that from this spot not one foot's space
of ground shall I give up. I shall go onwards,
in the fight avenge my friend and lord.
My deeds shall give no warrant for words of blame
to steadfast men on Stour, now he is stretched lifeless
– that I left the battlefield a lordless man,
turned for home. The irons shall take me,
point or edge.'

               Angrily he strode forth
and fought very fiercely; flight was beneath him.

Dart brandished, Dunnere spoke,
bidding his brothers avenge Bryhtnoth.
The humble churl called out over all:

'A man cannot linger when his lord lies
unavenged among Vikings, cannot value breath.'

So the household companions, careless of life,
bore spears to battle and set to bitter fighting:
they went out into the press, praying God
that among their enemies they might so acquit themselves
as to redress the death of their dear lord.

The hostage lent them help willingly;
he was a Northumbrian of a hard-fighting clan,
the son of Edgeleave, Ashferth his name;
wavered not at the war-play, but, while he might,
shot steadily from his sheaf of arrows,
striking a shield there, or shearing into a man,
and every once in a while wounding wryly.

At that time Long Edward still led the attack,
breathing his readiness, rolling out boasts
that nothing would budge him now that the best man lay,
nothing force him to flee one foot of ground.
He broke the board-wall, burst in among them,
wrought on the sea-wreckers a revenge worthy
his goldgiving lord before the ground claimed him.

So did the noble Aetheric, another of our company,
he too fought fixedly, furious to get on,
Sibyrht's brother; and so did many another,
cleaving in halves the hollow shields.
Board's border burst asunder,
corselet sang its chilling song.
How they beat off the blows!

                        At the battle's turn
Offa sent a seafarer stumbling to the ground;
but crippling strokes crashed down
and Gadd's kinsman was grounded also.

Yet Offa had made good his given word,
the oath undertaken to his open-handed lord,
that either they should both ride back to the burg's
       stockade,
come home whole, or harry the Danes
till life leaked from them and left them on the field.
Thane-like he lay at his lord's hand.

Then was a splintering of shields, the sea-wolves coming on
in war-whetted anger. Again the spears
burst breast-lock, breached life-wall
of Wierd-singled men. Wistan went forth,
that Thurstan fathered, fought with the warriors
where they thronged thickest. Three he slew
before the breath was out of Offa's body.

It was a stark encounter, but they stood their ground –
the warriors in that fight, fought till wounds
dragged them down. The dead fell.
All the while Eadwold and Oswold his brother

cried on their kinsmen, encouraging them
to stand up under the stress, strike out the hour,
weaving unwavering the web of steel.
Then Bryhtwold spoke, shook ash-spear,
raised shield-board. In the bravest words
this hoar companion handed on the charge:

> 'Courage shall grow keener, clearer the will,
> the heart fiercer, as our force faileth.
> Here our lord lies levelled in the dust,
> the man all marred: he shall mourn to the end
> who thinks to wend off from this war-play now.
> Though I am white with winters I will not away,
> for I think to lodge me alongside my dear one,
> lay me down by my lord's right hand.'

Godric likewise gave them all heart,
Aethelgar's son, sending spears,
death-darts, driving on the Danish ranks;
likewise he forged foremost among them,
scattering blows, bowing at last.

That was not the Godric who galloped away....

WIDSITH

Widsith is the poem of a travelling minstrel who visits every court in greater Germania, crossing the continent from the North Sea and the Baltic to the Black Sea. It is a roll-call of tribes and their rulers, and tells of several heroic stories touched on in *Beowulf*. R. W. Chambers edited the poem, which cannot easily be understood without the help of his edition. 'In *Widsith*,' he wrote,

> we have a catalogue of some seventy tribes and of sixty-nine heroes, many of whom can be proved to have existed in the third, fourth, and fifth centuries of our era, and the latest of whom belong to the sixth century. Yet, although every chief whom we can date lived prior, not only to the conversion of the English to Christianity, but even to the completion of their settlement in Britain, this thoroughly heathen poem has come down to us in a transcript which some English monk made about the year 1000.

Widsith, 'the wide-traveller', accompanies Ealhhild, a Lombard princess, on her journey 'eastward from Angel' to the court of Eormanric the Goth. Ealhhild, the sister of Aelfwine, King of the Lombards, is made to marry Eormanric. But in fact the Gothic tyrant had been dead for two hundred years when Aelfwine (Alboin) was murdered in 573; and his court would have been somewhere between the Sea of Azov and the Danube. The geography of *Widsith* is legendary (apart from the placing of the tribes who lived on the coasts of the North Sea and the Baltic) and the chronology is elastic. Yet the poem has historic value; apart from a long interpolation (printed here in square brackets) and one or two textual muddles, the information given is an authentic reflection of Anglian memories of their continental home.

In the poem, Widsith tells of the countries he went through and of the heroes he met. For the most part, these names are given in lists, but there are some – the most famous – whose stories are more fully told: Offa the Angle; the Danes,

Hrothwulf and Hrothgar; Alboin the Lombard; Eormanric; and Eormanric's retinue, into which the most famous characters of Gothic history have been attracted – Eastgota, Theodoric, Widia and Hama.

On to this simple structure two considerable additions have been soldered – the first a list of the rulers of the Germanic tribes, the other a gratuitous supplement of biblical and other knowledge. This last interpolation, referred to above, was presumably made much later.

The catalogue of Germanic kings, beginning with the name of Attila, is ancient, and probably antedates the composition of *Widsith*. Although it has no particular relevance at the beginning of Widsith's recital, and there are inconsistencies between it and situations described in the poem, this mnemonic catalogue of the folk-founders adds completeness to what was always an evocation of the heroic world rather than an account of an actual journey. In the course of their wanderings until their ultimate settlement in the different parts of Europe, the members of the Germanic family of nations did not forget their kinship nor their common origins. An Anglian roll-call of dead lords was not confined to Anglian heroes. The successes of the Goths against the Roman Empire were the boast of the German peoples; even the Huns played a part in their legends, though they were not a Germanic tribe.

Widsith is like a list of the *dramatis personae* of all the Germanic heroic poems; to its audience every name was a name to conjure with. No *Who's Who* was necessary: these names were known in Iceland, in Wessex, on the Vistula and in the Viking settlement at the mouth of the Volga. To some of them we cannot supply a note; the poet's concluding advice to kings, that – if they wanted 'a name that should never die beneath the heavens' – they should give employment to poets, now sounds ironic. Yet we should not be reading this poem if there were not some truth in the claim.

The poem might be divided as follows:

Prologue: Widsith's journey with Ealhhild to the court of Eormanric, her future husband.

The Catalogue of Germanic Kings: The Traveller announces his qualifications and gets down to naming tribes and their founders. At the top of the German catalogue we find an unknown Hwala and Alexander the Great. The mnemonic list begins with Attila and ends with Offa. Apart from Huns, Goths, Greeks and Burgundians, all the tribes mentioned come from the coasts of the Baltic and the North Seas. The stories of Offa the Angle and of Hrothgar and Hrothwulf, the kings of the neighbouring Danes, are given more fully.

A Second Catalogue: Widsith repeats his credentials and lists the tribes he has visited, again beginning with Huns and Goths, and again showing his knowledge of the north-west corner of Europe. Guthere the Burgundian and Aelfwine (Alboin the Lombard) are singled out for praise.

The Interpolation (lines 75–87): Chambers suggests that a copyist of *Widsith* thought that its history and geography would not be complete without the mention of people who had since come within the horizon of common knowledge.

Ealhhild and Eormanric: A resumption of the story begun in the Prologue. Eormanric gives the minstrel a ring of extraordinary value, which Widsith presents to his lord, Eadgils, on his return to his own country. Ealhhild also gives Widsith a ring, and the singer spreads the fame of her generosity.

The Followers of Eormanric: A catalogue of the most famous names in Gothic history and legend, concluding with references to the enmity of the Goths and the Huns, and to Widia and Hama, whose names survived into late medieval Germanic poetry.

Epilogue: The lot of the *scop* (poet), and his usefulness to society.

Widsith

This is the testimony of Widsith,
                    traveller through
kindreds and countries;
                    in courts he stood often,
knelt for the lovely stone,
                    no living man more often.
Unlocks his word-hoard.
                    (He went from the Myrgings
where his children were princes
                    with the peace-weaver,
the fair Ealhhild.
                    That was his first journey.
They went east from Angel
                    to Eormanric's halls
– the ruthless troth-breaker.)

                    His telling began thus:
'Of the master-rulers the most part have been known to me
and I say that any leader, any lord whosoever,
must live right, and rule his lands the same
if he wishes to come to a king's chair.
Of them all Hwala was for a while the best;
but Alexandreas' empire, of all I have heard of,
stretched furthest, and his strength flourished
more than that of any on earth I have heard of.

Attila ruled the Huns, Eormanric the Goths,
Becca the Banings, the Burgundians Gifeca,
Kaiser the Creeks, Caelic the Finns,
Hagena the Holm-Riggs, Heoden the Gloms;
Witta ruled the Swaefe, Wada the Hælsings,
Meaca the Myrgings, Mearchealf the Hundings.

Theodric ruled the Franks, Thyle the Rondings,
Breca the Brondings, Billing the Werns;
Oswine ruled the Eows, and the Eats Getwulf,
Finn Folcwalding the Frisian kin,

Sigehere swayed the Sea-Danes long,
Hnaef the Hocings, Helm the Wulfings,
Wald the Woings, Wod the Thurings,
Saeferth the Secgan, the Swedes Ongentheow,
Shafthere the Ymbers, Sheafa the Longbeards,
Hun the Hetwars, Holen the Wrosns,
Ringweald was the name of the Raiders' chief.

Offa ruled Angel, Alewih the Danes;
he was of all these men the most courageous,
yet he did not outdo Offa in valour:
before all men Offa stands,
having in boyhood won the broadest of kingdoms;
no youngster did work worthier of an earl.
With single sword he struck the boundary
against the Myrgings where it marches now,
fixed it at Fifeldor. Thenceforward it has stood
between Angles and Swaefe where Offa set it.

Hrothgar and Hrothwulf held their bond
– father's brother and brother's son –
long after their victory over the Viking clan
when they made Ingeld's edge bow,
hewed down at Heorot the Heathobard troop.

So fared I on through foreign lands
over the ground's breadth. Both good and evil
I came to know there; of no kinship,
from family far, I followed many.
So I may sing, and stories tell;
I can in hall rehearse before the gathering
how men of kingly birth were kinglike towards me.

I was among the Huns and among the Hreth-Goths
among Swedes, among Geats, and among South Danes,
among Verns I was, among Vikings, and among Vendels,
among Gepids I was, among Wends, and among Gefflegs,
among Angles I was, among Swaefe, and among Aenenes,
among Saxons I was, among Seggs, and among Swordmen,

among Whalemen I was, among Deans, and among
                    War-Reams,
with the men of Throndheim I was, and with Thuringians,
and among the Burgundians. I got there a ring,
Guthere gave me the gleaming token,
a bright stone for a song. He was not slow to give.
With Franks I was, with Frisians, and among Frumtings,
with Rugians I was, with Gloms, and among Rome-Welsh.

I was with Aelfwine in Italy too.
In my wanderings I've not met with a man whose hand
faster framed a fame-winning deed,
or who gave rings with gladder face
than Eadwin's bairn did the bright arm-bands.

[Among Saracens I was, and among Serings I was,
among Finns, among Creeks, and with Kaiser I was,
who was the wielder of wine-filled cities,
and rent and riches, and the Roman domain.
I was with Picts and with Scots and with Sliding-Finns,
with Leons and with Bretons and with Langobards,
with heathens and with heroes and with Hundings,
with the Israelites I was, and with the Exsyringians,
with Ebrews, with Indians, and with the Egyptians,
among Medes I was, and with Persians, with Myrgings,
and with the Mofdings *against* the Myrgings,
and among Amothings. With East Thuringians I was,
with Eols and with Ests and among Idumings.]

And I was with Eormanric all the days
that the Goth King was kind towards me:
lord over cities and they who lived in them.
Six hundred shillings' worth of sheer gold
were wound into the ring he reached to my hand.
(I owed it to Eadgils, overlord of the Myrgings,
my king and keeper, and at my coming home
I gave it to him against a grant of land
formerly bestowed on me, the estate of my father.)

Ealhhild also, before all the company
gave me another, Eadwin's daughter;
and when the name was asked of the noblest girl,
gold-hung queen, gift-dealer,
beneath the sky's shifting – the most shining lady –
I sang Ealhhild; in every land
I spoke her name, spread her fame.
When we struck up the lay before our lord in war,
Shilling and I, with sheer-rising voices,
the song swelling to the sweet-touched harp,
many men there of unmelting hearts,
who well knew, worded their thought,
said this was the best song sung in their hearing.

I travelled through every quarter of the kingdoms of the
                          Goths,
kept company only with clear-headed men.
Such might always be found among the fellows of
                          Eormanric.
Hethca I sought out, Beadeca, and the Herelings:
I found Emerca and Fridla, and Eastgota
the father of Unwen, no fool but a good man.
I came to Secca and Becca, was with Seafola and Theodoric,
Heathoric and Sifeca, Hlitha and Ongentheow.
I sought Eadwine, Elsa, Aegelmund, Hungar,
and the brave band of the Broad-Myrgings.
Wulfhere I sought, and Wormhere; war did not often
                          slacken there
when the Gothic host with hard swords
had to defend in the forests of the Vistula
their ancient hearthland against Attila's people.

I sought out Raedhere, Rondhere, Rumstan and Gislhere.
Withergield and Freotheric, and Widia and Hama,
– the worst of comrades they were not either,
though I have not named them first.
Whining and whistling, wooden shafts
streamed from their company, stooped on the enemy.

It was Widia and Hama who wielded the people,
two strangers distributed the gold.

In faring the roads I have found this true,
that among earth-dwellers the dearest men
are those whom God lends his lordship over others.'

The makar's wierd is to be a wanderer:
the poets of mankind go through the many countries,
speak their needs, say their thanks.
Always they meet with someone, in the south lands or the
                              north,
who understands their art, an open-handed man
who would not have his fame fail among the guard
nor rest from an earl's deeds before the end cuts off
light and life together.
                    Lasting honour shall be his,
a name that shall never die beneath the heavens.

Notes

The standard library edition of these texts remains *The Anglo-Saxon Poetic Records*, edited by G. P. Krapp and E. V. K. Dobbie, 6 vols. (New York and London, 1931–54), known as *ASPR*. The *ASPR* text was used in the facing-text edition of *The Earliest English Poems* published by the University of California Press in 1969. Most of the translations are based on texts from the Exeter Book. In finalizing my translations, I made use of *ASPR* III, *The Exeter Book* (1936), and followed its readings except where noted.

As I worked on the translations, however, I had three books open on my desk. One was the Early English Text Society edition of *The Exeter Book*, Part II, edited by W. S. Mackie (London, 1934). The others were the two unwieldy volumes of the venerable *An Anglo-Saxon Dictionary*, edited by Joseph Bosworth and T. N. Toller (Oxford, 1898, 1921). I made much use also of individual editions of single texts, especially the editions originally in Methuen's Old English Library, now published by Exeter University Press. Some more recent editions have also been consulted, including Bernard J. Muir's *The Exeter Anthology of Old English Poetry*, 2 vols., 2nd edn (Exeter, 2000) and *A Guide to Old English*, edited by Bruce Mitchell and Fred C. Robinson, 6th edn (Oxford, 2001), which has effectively replaced Sweet's *Anglo-Saxon Primer* and *Reader* as an introductory textbook.

The following books (full details given above) are referred to in an abbreviated form throughout the Notes:

ASPR – *The Anglo-Saxon Poetic Records*
Bosworth and Toller – *An Anglo-Saxon Dictionary*, edited by J. Bosworth and T. N. Toller
Mackie – *The Exeter Book*, Part II, edited by W. S. Mackie

Quotations from Tacitus' *Germania* are from the translation by
H. S. Mattingly in *Tacitus on Britain and Germany* (Harmondsworth,
1960). Please note that all line references are to the Old English text
rather than to the translations. Explanations of archaisms used more
than once in the translations, together with various words in Old
English that have been used 'neat', may be found in A Note on the
Translation (p. xxxiii).

THE RUIN (p. 1)

The text is damaged by fire. Translations of defective lines are in part
conjectural.

l. 4 I read *hrim geat berofen, hrim on lime*, accepting the repetition
      of *hrim*, but not of *torras* from l. 3. Some details of the initial
      description are close to the wording of the lamentations of Jere-
      miah over the ruins of Jerusalem, especially Chapter 2.
l. 12 I read *wonað giet se wealstan wæpnum geheawen* with
      Mackie.
l. 18 *hygerof* seems to imply some such interpretation of the first part
      of the line.
l. 22 *horngestreon* 'with a wealth of gables'. The hall-gables were
      often made to appear more fearsome by means of horn-
      ornaments. Heorot in *Beowulf* may have been so adorned
      (*heorot*: hart).
l. 26 Mackie suggests that *secgrof* may be the equivalent of Latin
      robur.
l. 31 I follow Mackie's reading.

GNOMIC VERSES (p. 5)

B. C. Williams's *Gnomic Poetry in Anglo-Saxon* (New York, 1914)
gave some hints.

Headnote

1. Some charms are translated in S. A. J. Bradley's *Anglo-Saxon
    Poetry* (London, 1982).
2. A. D. Hope's translation can be found in the essay 'Poetry and
    Platitude' in his *The Cave and the Spring* (Sydney, 1965).

l. 78 *deop deada wæg*: this could also mean 'the deep way of the dead'; in any case it is parallel with *sund unstille*.

l. 82 See Tacitus, *Germania*, 18:

> The dowry is brought by husband to wife, not by wife to husband. Parents and kinsmen attend and approve of the gifts, gifts not chosen to please a woman's whim or gaily deck a young bride, but oxen, horse with reins, shield, spear and sword. For such gifts a man gets his wife, and she in her turn brings some present of arms to her husband. In this interchange of gifts they recognize the supreme bond, the holy mysteries, the presiding deities of marriage.

l. 95 The Frisians are always presented as seafarers.

THE EXETER RIDDLES (p. 9)

Mackie's bilingual text and numbering of the riddles was followed. Other editions, including *ASPR*, are numbered differently. When preparing the larger selection which appears in my *Old English Riddles from the Exeter Book* (Anvil Press, London, 1980), I also used A. J. Wyatt's *Old English Riddles* (Boston, 1912). Anvil brought out a second edition of this book in 2007, with two new riddles, and a much enlarged introduction, which appears, with some differences, as the headnote to the Exeter Riddles in the present volume.

Headnote

1.   Chapter 2, verse 19 in the Douai version, which translates from the Latin Vulgate Bible used by the Anglo-Saxons.

Riddle 12. ASPR quotes the end of a riddle by Eusebius which makes it obvious that Riddle 12 is borrowed from Latin models.

ll. 4, 8 'Welsh' in Anglo-Saxon meant simply 'foreigner'; the Romans are 'Rome-Welsh'. Tyroleans refer to Italians as Welsh. The walnut, coming from Italy, was called a 'welsh nut'. However, there is no reason to suppose that the Welsh serfs referred to here were not Britons.

Riddle 26. The solution is obvious. There are several Latin analogues to this riddle, and a riddle by Tatwine which apparently parallels the Christian development here, though no direct translation can be shown.

l. 8 I have adopted the *ASPR* suggestion that Grein's insertion of *sprengde* before *speddropum* is not necessary, as one can take *geond* with *mec*.

l. 17 *nales dol wite*: Bosworth and Toller show that *dol* was used in the senses 'dull, foolish, erring, heretical'.

Riddle 27. For the reference to honey in l. 5, compare Riddle 79.

Riddle 30. Wood is the solution given, but it has not quite the same applications as the Old English *beam*, which can mean 'tree', 'ship', 'log', 'harp', 'cup', 'cross'. I do not follow Blackburn in thinking that 'ship' is meant in l. 3a – a branch of a tree could be *fus forðweges* – or that a harp is referred to in l. 5, where 'cup' would be more natural. The last lines of this riddle contain the idea which is the heart of *The Dream of the Rood* (see the headnote to that section).

Riddle 35. This warlike riddle translates Aldhelm's Latin *De Lorica*.

Riddle 38. Compare Riddle 12.

Riddle 42. The runes (see A Note on Runes) spell out *hana* and *hæn* – cock and hen.

Riddle 57. The last half-line, *nemnað hy sylfe*, may mean 'they name themselves' – i.e. that the birds' names are formed from their characteristic call. Jackdaws and crows have been proposed.

Riddle 60. A variation upon *Arundo* (Reed) of Symphosius, which alludes to the story of Syrinx in Ovid's *Metamorphoses*. Compare *The Husband's Message*.

Riddle 68. The first two lines of this riddle and the third and last line are written out in the Exeter Book as two separate riddles, of which the first is probably incomplete. I have, for simplicity's sake, translated the three lines as one riddle; but l. 3, taken on its own, makes good sense.

Riddle 69. Though *singeð þurh sidan* seems to indicate a wind instrument, *ASPR* notes that 'the description in lines 2b–4a seems to favour "harp"'. However, a shepherd's pipe is more likely to have been hung up by the wayside than a harp. Cf. Virgil, *Eclogues*, vii, 24.

Riddle 73. See the new solution, Snow, proposed by A. R. V. Cooper in *Agenda*, vol. 19, no. 1. 'A singular man' is masculine singular, a grammatical description of the word for snow in Old English.

Riddle 75. See the discussion in the headnote to the Exeter Riddles.

Riddle 79. As explained in the Note on the Translation, the opening exclamation is the Old English poet's call for attention: 'Listen!' It is a standard beginning for a poem, as in *Beowulf*, and especially appropriate here. Line 6 is a reference to the honey in the mead. Horn was used for many purposes in Anglo-Saxon times.

Riddle 80. The last line and a half are damaged by fire. I have translated Holthausen's *ond ic þæt þolian sceal/forþon ic wrecan ne mæg wonsceaft mine*; this was before I read the *ASPR* observation that this emendation was too long. However, the *ASPR ne ic wepan mæg* could just as easily read *wrecan*.

Riddle 85. A translation from Symphosius' Riddle 95, *luscus allium vendens*.

THE DREAM OF THE ROOD (p. 30)

I used throughout the text of Bruce Dickins and A. S. C. Ross in their edition originally in Methuen's Old English Library. The text also appears in Sweet's *Reader* and in Mitchell and Robinson's *Guide to Old English*. Aspects of the poem not fully covered in Dickins and Ross are dealt with in articles by H. R. Patch ('Liturgical Influence in *The Dream of the Rood*', PMLA, xxiv, pp. 233–57) and R. Woolf ('Doctrinal Influences on *The Dream of the Rood*', *Medium Aevum*, vol. 27, no. 3, 1958). The comprehensive edition by Michael Swanton (Manchester, 1970) supersedes Dickins and Ross; its introduction is especially useful on the cult of the Cross from Constantine's original vision onwards. On the relation of the stone cross and the Vercelli text, see Éamonn Ó Carragáin's *Ritual and the Rood* (London, 2005).

l. 8 I interpret with Sweet, though Patch's suggestion (that *foldan sceatum* means the corners of the earth, and that the Rood is here thought of as reaching out to them) is attractive. *Eorðan sceatas* in l. 37 refers to the earth's surface.

l. 8 'five stones': Patch mentions the occurrence of crosses with five jewels in early mosaics. The five grains of incense, symbolic of the Five Wounds, placed in the Paschal Candle might also have suggested this.

l. 13 *sigebeam*: Patch quotes several references from the Liturgy to the *lignum triumphale*, for example the famous hymn *Vexilla regis prodeunt*. Woolf notes that Christ is presented in this poem as *Christus miles*, the champion who conquers death. It is only in the later Middle Ages that the suffering and pathos of the Crucifixion are emphasized more than this heroic aspect. The word *signum*, used in the translation, is Latin for 'standard', 'sign'.

l. 15 *wædum geweorðod*: I have taken this as parallel to *gegyred mid golde*. *Wædum* (weeds) usually means 'clothing', but Bosworth and Toller seem to allow this meaning.

l. 19 *earmra*: cf. *fracodes* in l. 10.

l. 22 Patch's explanation is plausible: the alternation of gold and blood is related to the two natures in the single person of Christ (the human, which can suffer, the divine, which cannot) – reflected in the change of colour of the vestments on Palm Sunday, when the red cross of Lent gives way to a more ornamental cross.

l. 26 *þæt*: 'how', as Sweet notes.

l. 36 this echoes Matthew 27: 51: *terra mota est et petrae scissae sunt*: 'The earth quaked and the rocks were rent'.

l. 39 *hæleð*: hero. The assimilation of the New Testament story into Germanic terms is complete. In line 42 and elsewhere the Cross refuses to disobey its lord.

ll. 55–6 'All creation wept': Dickins and Ross cite the parallel of all creation weeping to rescue Baldr from Hel in the Norse prose *Eddas*.

l. 63 Woolf notes that it is nowhere said that Christ died.

l. 76 Referring to the Invention of the Cross by the Empress Helena, Constantine's mother.

ELEGIES (p. 46)

For *The Wanderer* I have used the *ASPR* text, except where noted. *The Seafarer* is edited separately in Methuen's Old English Library by I. L. Gordon, on whose text I have relied. Sweet's *Reader* and Mitchell and Robinson contain both poems, Mackie *The Seafarer* only. Both were well translated by N. Kershaw in *Anglo-Saxon and Norse Poems* (Cambridge, 1922). *ASPR* ends the first speech in *The Wanderer* at l. 29a. I end it at l. 63, as does Sweet's *Reader*. Mitchell and Robinson do not divide the text into speeches. Bernard J. Muir's *Exeter Anthology of Old English Poetry*, 2 vols., 2nd edn (Exeter, 2000), gives references to biblical passages and commentaries with wording very close to passages in these poems. I added prose translations of the devotional conclusion of *The Seafarer*, and of the second half of *The Dream of the Rood*, in the second edition of *The Earliest English Poems*.

The Wanderer (p. 51)

l. 1 *gebideð* can mean either 'expects', 'waits for' or 'lives to experience'. This last 'perfective' sense is well attested, and has become the established interpretation. The different conclusion I came to when making this translation in 1961 remains compatible with the Boethian/Christian approach offered in the introduction to these two poems.

l. 6 *eardstapa*: wanderer. It is also the term for a grasshopper, literally 'homeland-stepper'.

l. 27 I accept Klaeber's insertion of *min* before *mine wisse*.

ll. 42–3 This probably refers to some ritual of fealty.

l. 53 *eft* makes better sense than *oft*.

ll. 70–72 It was customary to boast at the ale-drinking of the feats one would perform in battle; see *Maldon*, 212, where the noble Aelfwine reminds his companions of the 'battle-vows on the bench'.

l. 87 'giant-works': see the headnote to *The Ruin*.

The Seafarer (p. 55)

l. 1 Compare the opening of *The Wife's Lament*.

l. 16 The second half of this line is presumed to have been omitted by accident.

ll. 19–24 I. L. Gordon ornithologizes. Concurring with Margaret Goldsmith that 'we cannot identify all the species exactly, since from the evidence of glosses it appears that the Anglo-Saxons did not make the clear distinctions between the species that are made now', she remarks on *huilpan* (l. 21):

> Miss Daunt (MLR xiii. 478) and Miss Kershaw would identify the bird as the bar-tailed godwit or 'yarwhelp'. But both the modern English and Scottish dialect *whaup* and the cognate Low German forms, such as Dutch *wulp*, Frisian *wilp*, are used of the curlew (see *NED* under *whaup*) and this is pretty clearly the generic sense, the godwit being called 'yarwhelp' because it resembles the curlew.

Many curlews are summer visitors only, but there are always some
that remain round our coast in winter.

ll. 24–5 The translation condenses the Old English, the repetition of
isigfeðera and *urigfeðera*, and the lack of alliteration in l. 25
indicating that the text is corrupt.

l. 26 Grein's *frefran*, comfort, for *feran*, is convincing.

l. 33 *corna caldast*: 'coldest of grains'. My translation conserves the
visual side of the image. I. L. Gordon shows that there is reason
to think that this was a magical formula, the hailstones being
thought of as seeds of winter. See also A Note on Runes.

l. 40 *ne his gifena þæs god*: 'nor so well endowed'.

l. 53 The cuckoo is thought of as bringing sorrow both here and in
The Husband's Message, whereas elsewhere in Germanic litera-
ture the cuckoo is the harbinger of spring (as well as of cuck-
oldry). The cuckoo is a bird of lament in Welsh poetry, and
for the probable Welsh influence on the elegies I. L. Gordon's
introduction (pp. 15–18) should be read.

l. 81 My translation is a variation on Pound's 'and all arrogance of
earthen riches', which cannot be bettered, although *rices* does
not mean 'riches'. (See 'The Seafarer' in Ezra Pound, *Selected
Poems 1908–1959*, London, 1975.)

ll. 97–102 I read *wille* with the MS and *ASPR*.

LOVE POEMS (p. 59)

I have relied upon the *ASPR* introduction, text and notes, and have
found Mackie's translations useful. N. Kershaw's *Anglo-Saxon and
Norse Poems* (Cambridge, 1922) contains excellent translations.

The Wife's Lament (p. 62)

l. 15 *herheard*: I follow the majority of editors in dividing this as
her heard, but Grein suggested, very plausibly, that we should
read *herh-eard*, meaning a dwelling in a (sacred) grove.

l. 24 There is an omission after *nu* in the Old English text.

l. 42 I take these lines on the *smylere* as directed against the person
responsible for the estrangement – the Iago of this affair.

The Husband's Message (p. 65)

ll. 1–7   Only a limited reconstruction is possible, but it is obvious that the staff is giving its personal history previous to this errand.

ll. 32–9   Translated along the lines suggested in the *ASPR* notes. It is fair to guess that the word omitted before 'of men' was *holdra*; the implication being that the husband had enough loyal followers to tell his wife to come.

l. 48   I have taken *ofer* as meaning 'over and above', and hope to have implied this in the syntax. A new sentence seems to begin with *gecyre*.

l. 50   See A Note on Runes for a proposed solution.

Wulf and Eadwacer (p. 68)

l. 9   *wenum dogode*: meaning either 'suffered from hopes of' or (if the emendation *hogode* is accepted) 'was thinking of'. The metre is odd, and I have taken the simpler meaning.

l. 16   *earne*: cowardly; or *eargne*: miserable. Both, I hope, are implied in 'whelp'.

HEROIC POEMS (p. 69)

Deor (p. 71)

The *ASPR* notes and text have been followed throughout. Kemp Malone's edition of the poem in Methuen's Old English Library (London, 1933) is convenient and informative.

l. 1   Malone suggests that *wurman* refers to the serpentine inlay upon the sword with which Wayland was maimed. The left panel on the front of the Franks Casket, a small carved whalebone box from early eighth-century Northumbria, given to the British Museum by Sir Augustus Franks in 1867, shows Wayland presenting a cup he has made out of a skull of one of the sons of his captor, Nithhad, to their father. Behind Nithhad stands his pregnant daughter Beadohild. Immediately next to this scene of triumphant vengeance, the right front panel shows the Adoration of the Magi. These violently contrasting panels show (a) the presentation of gifts, and (b) a pregnant woman whose child is to do great things: a pagan epiphany and the Christian Epiphany (see the front cover of this book). Other panels on the casket show a variety of scenes, not unlike those of *Deor*.

l. 6 *seonobende*: sinew-bonds, bonds caused by cutting the sinews.

l. 14 I read *mæð Hild* with Grein, and follow Mackie's interpretation. Hild and Geat (or *the* Geat), her lover, are unknown.

l. 18 This Theodoric may be Theodoric the Ostrogoth who ruled Verona (Bern, 'the Maering city') for 'only' thirty years before being exiled by Eormanic; or Theodoric the Frank who was exiled to Merano and ruled it unhappily for thirty years.

l. 36 Heodenings: the people ruled by Heoden. See note to *Widsith*, 21–2.

l. 37 Deor says he was *scop* of the Heodenings. The word *scop* corresponds to the Old Scots *makar*, poet.

Passages from *Beowulf* (p. 73)

The text followed is that of *Beowulf: A Glossed Text*, edited by Michael Alexander (Harmondsworth, 2nd edn, 2005).

The Funeral of Scyld Shefing: lines 26–52 (p. 75)

l. 44 'not less great': that is, much greater, for Scyld had arrived with nothing. This extreme understatement, known as litotes, is characteristic of Old English verse.

l. 48 *signum*: Old English *segen* is one of a dozen Latin-derived words in *Beowulf*. See also *The Dream of the Rood*, 13 *n*.

Beowulf's Voyage to Denmark: lines 194–257 (p. 77)

l. 199 'the warrior king': Hrothgar.

l. 203 'hardly or not at all': typical litotes. The elders encouraged Beowulf in his idea.

l. 204 'watched omens': a reference which places the action in a pre-Christian time.

l. 224 'Weather-Geats': the *Geatas* are sometimes called *Weder-Geatas* (Storm-dwelling Geats; *Weder*, storm) or *Wederas*. The Geats are seafarers, Vikings.

l. 247 'word of leave from Hrothgar and Hrothwulf': Hrothwulf is Hrothgar's sister's son, and has a share in the rule of the Danes.

To Grendelsmere and Back: lines 837–75 (p. 79)

l. 837 *mine gefræge*: 'as I have heard tell'; the traditional formula.
l. 840 'the wonder': Grendel's arm, which Beowulf has torn off and
placed on one of the gables of Heorot.
l. 842 'not . . . one man sorry': litotes again.
l. 871 *soðe gebunden*: 'truly bound together' – i.e. by alliteration.
Editors have compared *Sir Gawain and the Green Knight* 35 –
with lel letteres loken: 'locked together with loyal letters'.
l. 874 *wordum wrixlan*: 'rang word-changes'. A reference to poetic
variation.
l. 875 *Sigemunde*: the *scop* is made to compare Beowulf with the
greatest of all the dragon-slayers of Germanic tradition, Sige-
mund in the English tradition, Siguthur in the Old Icelandic
Eddas and in the Volsung Sagas, Siegfried in the *Nibelungenlied*.
Sigemund slays the treasure-guarding dragon, but the hoard has
a death-curse upon it. Beowulf's own end is foreshadowed.

The Lament of the Last Survivor: lines 2231–66 (p. 81)

l. 2241 The barrow is situated on a headland, like the barrow in
which the ashes of Beowulf himself are to be buried.

The Fight at Finnsburgh (p. 85)

The text followed is that of George Jack's *Beowulf: A Student Edition*
(Oxford, 1994), though I read *wealle* in l. 28 and *hwearf blacra hraes*
in l. 34.

l. 43 The wounded warrior seems best understood as one of the
attackers, and the 'folk's shepherd' (l. 45) as Finn.

The Battle of Brunanburgh (p. 89)

The edition followed is that of John C. Pope in *Seven Old English
Poems*, 2nd edn (New York, 1981).

l. 1 Athelstan: King of Wessex, Mercia and England, 924–39.
l. 3 Edmund: aged sixteen at the time of the battle, king 939–46.
l. 6 'leavings of hammers': swords.
l. 7 Edward: the Elder, Alfred's eldest son, king 899–924.
l. 11 'shipmen': Vikings.
l. 18 'Northerners': Vikings.

l. 26 Anlaf: Olaf Guthfrithson of Dublin.
l. 28 'five kings': other annals confirm this.
l. 30 'earls': Norse *jarls*.
l. 32 'scant': that is, no.
l. 33 'Prince': Anlaf.
l. 36 'slipped away': that is, disgracefully.
l. 37 'The Old King': Constantine III of Scots.
l. 44 'yield': that is, the slaughter.
l. 45 'chieftain': Constantine.
l. 55 'Dingsmere': the Irish Sea.
l. 69 'since': that is, since the fifth century.

The Battle of Maldon (p. 95)

I have used E. V. Gordon's edition, revised by D. G. Scragg and published by Manchester University Press in 1976. The text is also to be found in Sweet's *Reader*, and Mitchell and Robinson. E. D. Laborde's article in the *English Historical Review*, vol. 40 (1925), pp. 161 ff., successfully identified the site of the battle. D. G. Scragg, *The Return of the Vikings: The Battle of Maldon 991* (Oxford, 2007) was published too late to be consulted.

l. 2 'He' is Bryhtnoth. Fighting was done on foot, and the sending away of the horses shows that there was no intention of retreat.
l. 5 Offa seems to have been Bryhtnoth's second-in-command, and leads the English after the earl's death.
l. 6 *se eorl*: Bryhtnoth. The word *eorl* is derived from Scandinavian *jarl*, and is here used in its fullest sense of Ealdorman, or ruler of the East Saxons. Elsewhere, 'earl' is often a synonym for 'warrior'. Bryhtnoth was one of the most powerful Ealdormen of his day, both in lands and in personal influence, and is historically important as one of the most vigorous supporters of the reform of the monasteries and the friend of three successive kings. The historian of the monastery of Ely, to which Bryhtnoth gave much land, records in the twelfth century that 'He was eloquent, robust, of great bodily stature . . . and remarkably brave and free from the fear of death'. He seems to have made a great impression on his age. All the evidence corroborates the picture given of him in the poem – that he was pious, impetuous, an experienced war-leader, and that his hair was 'swan-white'. E. V. Gordon, from whose introduction this information is taken, has calculated that at the time of the battle he would have been sixty-five or

more. I reproduce an account he cites of the investigation of Bryhtnoth's tomb in Ely Cathedral, where his remains had been transferred from Ely Abbey at the time of the Ely historian. This history relates that the Abbot and monks of Ely carried Bryhtnoth's body from the field after the battle, but that his head had been cut off and taken away by the Vikings. A letter read before the Society of Antiquaries in 1772 confirms this story, and also the tradition that he was of a gigantic height:

> I apprised those who attended on that occasion, 18 May 1769, that if my surmises were well-founded no head would be found in the cell which contained the Bones of Brithnoth, Duke of Northumberland . . . (Under the effigy of) Duke Brithnoth there were no remains of the head, though we searched diligently, and found most, if not all his other bones almost entire, and those remarkable for their length, and proportionally strong; which also agrees with what is recorded by the same historian with regard to the Duke's person, viz. that he was *viribus robustus, corpore maximus* . . . It was estimated . . . that the Duke must have been 6 feet 9 inches in stature. It was observed that the collar-bone had been nearly cut through, as by a battle-axe or two-handed sword.

l. 24 *heorðwerod*: this is the *comitatus* of Tacitus: 'not chance or the accident of mustering makes the troop or wedge, but family and friendship, and this is a very powerful incitement to valour', *Germania*, 7. The *heorðwerod* are distinguished from the *fyrd*, or local levy, who have to be taught how to stand.

l. 29 The Viking spokesman addresses his words both to 'thee' and 'you'. As E. V. Gordon says, 'there seems to be no difficulty in taking the singular as applying specifically to Bryhtnoth and the plural to the English generally'.

l. 42 The raising of the shield was to call for silence. There is no reason to suppose that the poetic convention does not mirror an actual convention.

l. 51 *unforcuð*: 'not the meanest'. This is not the literal meaning; but litotes (extreme understatement) is a common trick in Old English verse.

l. 66 *lucon lagustreamas*: 'the sea's arms locked' – a description, as Laborde suggests, of the tide joining around the western end of Northey Island; this could have been seen by both sides quite clearly.

l. 75 Wulfstan may have been specially chosen to defend the *brycg* because the battle was being fought on his land. His son Leofwine leaves the land of Purleigh near the site of the battle, in his will, and Domesday makes no mention of land between Purleigh and the estuary, so the inference is probable.

l. 77 *francan*: Frankish spears were esteemed; but, as E. V. Gordon shows, the word has lost any very precise denotation, being used interchangeably with *gar*. Here Wulfstan throws it; but in l. 140 Bryhtnoth clearly thrusts it into his man.

l. 91 *ceallian ofer cald wæter*: cold is always baleful. All the destructive runes are connected with winter.

l. 98 'sheer': I modernize the spelling of *scir*, in the hope that the ghost of the proper meaning – 'shining' – might still lurk in the word.

l. 102 'war-hedge': the men in the second rank held their shields above their heads to protect the men in front as well as themselves. Ideally the shields overlapped, so that there would be no chink.

l. 106 Ravens occur in *Finnsburgh*, 34 (translated, I fear, into 'crows'), and in most Northern poems before battles.

l. 115 *swustersunu*: cf. *Widsith*, 45 *n*.; also Tacitus, *Germania*, 20.

l. 134 *superne*: cf. *francan*, l. 77.

l. 169 *har hilderinc*: *cigneam canitiem sui capitis* of the *Vita Oswaldi*.

l. 181 'heathen churls': the opprobrium lay in the adjective.

l. 217 Aelfwine is with Bryhtnoth, as E. V. Gordon says, because he has been expelled from his patrimony. Tacitus: 'Many noble youths, if the land of their birth is stagnating in a protracted peace, deliberately seek out other tribes, where some war is afoot', *Germania*, 14. This would apply to Beowulf's setting out for Denmark better than to the present passage, however.

l. 251 'lordless': Tacitus: 'Men have often survived battle only to end their shame by hanging themselves', *Germania*, 6.

l. 255 Dunnere's speech is very short, which is perhaps fitting for a yeoman among the household companions. However, Leofsunu, who speaks for longer, does not seem to be of noble birth.

l. 265 The hostage is traditionally more loyal even than the lord's own retainers; cf. the hostage in the story of Cynewulf and Cyneheard in the *Anglo-Saxon Chronicle*.

l. 266 Bryhtnoth is described in the *Liber Eliensis* as *Northanimbrorum dux*, and he may have had some connection with Northumbria (as well as Mercia; see note above). See l. 6 *n*.

l. 300 I agree with E. V. Gordon that *Wigelmes bearn* must refer to Offa, and have substituted his name for clarity's sake.

l. 309 Bryhtwold may be a retainer, or a close kinsman. See the
        Glossary of Proper Names.

Widsith (p. 108)

In his edition of *Widsith* (Cambridge, 1912), R. W. Chambers dis-
cussed very fully the historical and ethnographical features of the
poem. My headnote (see p. 105) and the facts contained in the notes
below and in the Glossary of Proper Names owe a great debt to him.
The *ASPR* text and notes are followed.

l. 5 *Ealhhild*: this daughter of Eadwin (l. 74) is apparently the sister
      of Alboin the Lombard (l. 99), and her marriage to Eormanric is
      meant to form a bond between Lombards and Goths. The
      Lombards lived on the lower Elbe, immediately next to the
      Myrgings and the Angles, before moving south into Italy. It is
      possible that she is to be identified with the Sunilda of the Latin
      historian Jordanes, a woman whom Eormanric orders to be torn
      in half by horses as a punishment for the revolt of her husband.
      See R. W. Chambers, pp. 15 ff.
l. 8 *eastan of Ongle*: 'from the East, from Angel'.
l. 9 *wraþes wærlogan*: Eormanric is a tyrant in *Deor* and in some later
      tradition; he is presented in *Widsith* as extraordinarily generous.
      Greatness and generosity were associated. The reputation for
      cruelty may come, R. W. Chambers suggests, from the sentence
      of death passed on Sunilda (see above).
ll. 21–2 The story of Hagen and Heoden is one of the most popu-
      lar of Germanic tales. R. W. Chambers quotes the four complete
      versions of it extant, and shows that the mention of Wade in
      the next line is not accidental. Wade was a sea-giant, a super-
      natural not an historic character, though he has here become
      the King of the Hælsings. The core of the story is that Heoden
      loves Hild, the daughter of King Hagen, and sends Heorrenda,
      his minstrel, to woo for him. Heorrenda's magic song per-
      suades the girl to escape, and she and Heorrenda flee to Heoden's
      court in Wade's magic boat. Hagen pursues his daughter, and he
      and his men fight Heoden and his followers (on the island of
      Hoy, in the Orkneys, according to Snorri Sturluson). Hagen is
      killed.

      Heorrenda occurs in *Deor* as the poet who replaces Deor at
      the court of the Heodenings. Wade's boat is mentioned in
      Chaucer's *The Merchant's Tale* and also in *Troilus*, when

Pandare 'tolde tale of Wade' to Criseyde. Chambers cannot add much to Speght's celebrated note in his edition of Chaucer (1598): 'Concerning Wade and his bote called Guingelot, as also his strange exploits in the same, because the matter is long and fabulous, I passe it over.'

ll. 25–8 All the tribes mentioned here were neighbours of the Angles in South Jutland.

l. 35 *Offa weold Ongle*: this praise of Offa the Angle, inappropriate in the mouth of a Myrging *scop*, is a reason for thinking that *Widsith* was composed or revised in the reign of Offa of Mercia, his descendant in the twelfth generation if we are to believe the genealogies. Offa here is the founder of Angel. The story referred to is told, with variations, by two Danish historians at the end of the twelfth century, Sweyn Aageson and Saxo Grammaticus. It is the story of Offa's duel on the island of Fifeldor at the mouth of the Eider against two Myrgings – the Prince of the Swaefe, and a chosen champion. The 'single sword' is an important part of this dramatic tale, summarized in R. W. Chambers's introduction.

ll. 45–50 ff. These five lines refer to the famous alliance between two members of the house of Scyld, the Scylding family which ruled the Danes. In *Beowulf*, Hrothwulf is the son of Halga, Hrothgar's younger brother. Hrothgar favoured his famous nephew greatly; between them they overcame (as is related here) the Heathobards under their chief, Ingeld.

Hrothgar married his daughter Freawaru to the young leader of the Heathobards, Ingeld, in the hope of healing an ancient feud between Danes and Heathobards in which Froda, Ingeld's father, had lost his life. At his return home, one of Ingeld's own retainers kills one of Freawaru's Danish followers; and the feud is resurrected again. In subsequent fighting at Heorot, Ingeld and his followers are slain.

A further tragic event in the history of the Scylding house is clearly foreshadowed in *lengest*; it is said that the kinsmen kept faith together 'for a very long time' after this famous victory. This seems to imply that the pact was eventually broken; Hrothwulf repays Hrothgar's generosity in fostering and protecting him – even to the point where he, the nephew, had eclipsed Hrothgar's own two sons – by murdering the sons and taking the Danish throne after the death of their father.

This truly laconic sentence, resuming the whole history of one generation of the Scylding house, is paralleled by the equally tight-lipped stanzas of *Deor*. Ingeld was popular enough in story for Alcuin, writing in 797 to the monks of Lindisfarne, to conclude his epistle (which recommends them to listen to the Scriptures and the doctrine of the Fathers of the Church rather than to the harp and to heathen songs) by the rhetorical question: '*Quid enim Hinieldus cum Christo?*' ('For what has Ingeld to do with Christ?' or 'What is Ingeld in comparison with Christ?').

l. 57 *Hreð-Gotum*: Hreth-Goths, another name for the Goths. Huns and Goths were traditionally enemies.

l. 63 The three tribes mentioned in this line probably lived in modern Norway.

ll. 65–7 Guthere (see Glossary of Proper Names) later became identified with the King of the Volsungs. See R. W. Chambers, pp. 58 ff.

ll. 75–87 The interpolated catalogue (see the headnote to this poem).

l. 83 Perhaps an attempt to reconcile passages like ll. 38–44, where the poet is apparently opposed to the Myrgings, with ll. 93–6.

l. 87 Probably three tribes inhabiting the Baltic provinces of Russia.

ll. 88–9 Or 'all of which time the Gothic King was kind towards me'.

l. 91 An arm-ring, not a finger-ring.

l. 93 Eadgils was probably an historical king of the Myrgings. It was his killing of an Anglian chief which started the feud terminated by Offa at Fifeldor (see l. 35 *n* and R. W. Chambers, pp. 92–4).

l. 104 'our lord in war': Eadgils.

ll. 112 ff. Hethca and Beadeca do not belong among the Gothic heroes. The Herelings are Emerca and Fridla, Eormanric's nephews, put to death by his order. Eastgota is the founder of the Ostrogothic fortunes. Seafola (Sabene) is Theodoric's faithful retainer. Sifeca persuaded Eormanric to murder the Herelings. Theodoric, the greatest of the Ostrogoths, was exiled (in legend) from Verona by Eormanric.

Finally we come to the legendary battle between the Goths and the Huns (under Attila) *ymb Wistlawudu* ('in the forests of the Vistula'). The Goths had left the Vistula by the end of the second century, and at that time Attila was unborn and the Huns unheard of. The long struggle between the peoples took place on the plains north of the Black Sea in the fourth century. But however unhistoric the chronology and geography of this passage, the antiquity of the saga-tradition it preserves can be felt. The wood – Mirkwood, as it is called in Icelandic legend – was the ancient heartland of the Goths. All the famous names of

Gothic story are ranged with Eormanric, in whose reign the threat of the Huns was first felt, and the Huns are led by their most feared leader, Attila.

The names in l. 123 all belong to the Gothic cycle, though the last, Gislhere, was a Burgundian. Freotheric may be Eormanric's son. Only with Wudga (Widia) and Hama do we emerge into the comparative clarity of often-recorded names; see the Glossary of Proper Names.

ll. 135–6 'makar': see *Deor*, 37 n.

A Note on Runes

The runic alphabet or *futhark* first came into being towards the end of the third century BC among the tribes of the South Tyrol, who combined their Italic script with various magic symbols or pictographs commonly in use among the Germanic peoples: these earlier symbols had been used for sortilege, or the casting of lots, a practice to which the Germans were addicted, according to Tacitus (*Germania*, 10; also *Beowulf*, 204). Runic inscriptions are found on weapons, coins and such objects as the Franks Casket throughout Europe north of the Alps, and although they were adopted for Christian purposes (as, for example, on the Ruthwell Cross), the Synod of Clofesho (747) still found it necessary to condemn divination.

Runes were originally conceived as signs to be carved, and never developed a cursive form. They were used for secret writing and for riddling; Cynewulf signs his poems with runes, as did the sender of *The Husband's Message*. One or two runes were adopted for the Old English alphabet – þ, for example, which is the sign at once for Thorn (which it resembles visually) and for the 'th' sound. This has survived into our own day as the 'Y' of Ye Olde Tea Shoppe. It is a characteristic irony that þ was, according to Elliott's *Runes*, the rune associated with the Gothic *thurisaz*, a demon, before it was given its more innocuous meaning of Thorn. For further information on the subject R. W. V. Elliott's *Runes: An Introduction* (Manchester, 1959, rev. 1989) should be consulted.

The Husband's Message ends:

> Gecyre ic ætsomme · ᚺ · ᚱ · geador
> · ᛉ · ᛈ · *ond* · ᛗ · aþe benemnan.
> þæt he þa wære · *ond* þa wintetreowe
> be him lifgendum · læstan wolde
> þe git on ærdagum · oft gespræcon

According to *ASPR* (see Notes, p. 113), the punctuation of the runes
in the MS indicates that they are to be read separately rather than in a
group or groups; two solutions are proposed in the *ASPR* Notes.
Elliott has given what seems to me a more convincing interpretation.
Taking the last rune as the M-rune rather than the D-rune, he gives
the message (somewhat expanded) as: 'Follow the *sun's path* (*sigel-
rad*) south across the *ocean* (*ear*) to find *joy* (*wyn*) with the *man* (*mon*)
who is waiting for you' (*Runes*, p. 73).

The anagram runes in Riddle 42 are used simply as shorthand, their
initial letters spelling out the solution. They are ᚠ, ᛉ, ᚱ and ᚻ; their
meanings are given in my translation.

Proposed Solutions to the Riddles

Glossary of Proper Names

This glossary is intended to be complete; the only names I have not glossed are those of the many tribes or heroes in *Widsith* about which nothing certain is known and the names in the translation of the historical poem *Brunanburgh* added in the third edition of *The Earliest English Poems*, which are glossed in the notes to that poem. Any other names occurring in the poems should be here.

AELFERE One of Wulfstan's companions at the *brycg*. *Maldon*, 80.

AELFNOTH A follower of Bryhtnoth who stood at his side in the battle. *Maldon*, 183.

AELFRIC Father of Aelfwine. Ealdorman of Mercia in 983, banished two years later for political reasons, and perhaps on that account omitted from Aelfwine's boast of his lineage. *Maldon*, 209.

AELFWINE Kinsman of Bryhtnoth, son of Aelfric and grandson to Ealhelm. *Maldon*, 211, 231.

AELFWINE The name given to Alboin, leader of Lombard invasion of Italy in 568 and the last of the Germanic conquerors of Rome. *Widsith*, 70 ff.

AETHELGAR Father of the Godric who did not flee at Maldon. *Maldon*, 320.

AETHELRED King of England 978–1016. He was the second King Aethelred. The literal meaning of the two components of his name – *æthel-ræd* – is 'noble and resourceful', but because of his repeated failure to withstand the Danish invasions he was known as *Æthelræd-unræd*. Hence the modern 'the Unready'. *Maldon*, 53, 151, 203.

AETHERIC One of Bryhtnoth's retainers, possibly the Aetheric who was later suspected of plotting to recognize Sweyn, the Viking, as King of Essex. Brother of Sibyrht. *Maldon*, 280.

ALEXANDREAS Alexander the Great (d. 323 BC). He later became the hero of cycles of romance. His mention at *Widsith*, 15, is not necessarily an interpolation.

ANGEL The continental home of the Angles, to the south of Jutland. *Widsith*, 8, 35.

ANGLES The continental Angles of Angel(n). *Widsith*, 44, 61. See also the end of *Brunanburgh*.

ASHFERTH Son of Edgeleave; a Northumbrian hostage of noble birth who fights bravely for Bryhtnoth. *Maldon*, 267.

ATTILA King of the Huns, conqueror of Rome, d. 453. Though not a German, celebrated in Germanic tradition in the company of Eormanric and Aelfwine (Alboin). *Widsith*, 18.

BEADOHILD The Bothvildr of the *Völundarkviða*, Nithhad's daughter. Wayland killed her two brothers and ravished her before escaping from Nithhad. She is cited in the second strophe of *Deor* as an example of misfortune outlived because the son born of this union was Widia, who became a great hero.

BECCA One of Eormanric's followers, ruler of the Banings. In legend, the evil counsellor who advised Eormanric to murder Sunilda. *Widsith*, 19, 115.

BEOWULF The protagonist of the poem. Son of Edgethew, nephew of the historical king of the Geats, Hygelac.

BRECA Ruler of the Brondings, as in *Beowulf*, where he has a five-day swimming match with the hero of the poem. *Widsith*, 25.

BRIGHTHELM Byrhtelm, father of Bryhtnoth. *Maldon*, 92.

BRYHTNOTH The English leader at Maldon, son of Byrhtelm. See Notes, pp. 124–5. In Old English his name is properly Byrhtnoth (battle-bright), but I have 'metathesized' the 'r' for euphony.

BURGUNDIANS An East Germanic tribe who later founded a kingdom in the Rhineland. Defeated by the opposition of Huns in the east and Gauls in the west. The central characters of some of the *Eddas*, the *Nibelungenlied* and Wagner's *Ring* come from the Burgundian royal house. Guthere is their leader. *Widsith*, 19, 65.

BYRHTWOLD The *eald geneat* of Bryhtnoth who speaks the famous lines beginning at *Maldon*, 213. Either a trusted retainer or (if he is identified with Bryhtwold, *cniht* of Aethelflaed, Bryhtnoth's widow) a member of the Ealdorman's closest personal following.

CEOLA Father of Wulfstan. *Maldon*, 76.

DANES Originally (e.g. in *Widsith*, 35) inhabitants of southern Sweden. When the Angles invaded England, the Danes crossed into the country now called after them. Hrothgar's people – the tribe best known in Anglian tradition. Bryhtnoth's Viking opponents at Maldon.

DUNNERE A simple churl who stands with the nobles of Bryhtnoth's household. *Maldon*, 255.

EADGILS Widsith's lord, chief of the Myrgings. See *Widsith*, 93 *n*.

EADRIC One of Bryhtnoth's retainers. *Maldon*, 11.

EADWIN Father of Aelfwine (Alboin) at *Widsith*, 74, and Ealhhild at *Widsith*, 99. King of the Lombards.

EADWOLD Retainer of Bryhtnoth, brother to Oswold. *Maldon*, 304.

EAHA One of Hnaef's followers at Finnsburgh. *Finnsburgh*, 15.

EALHELM Grandfather of Aelfwine, father-in-law of Aelfric Ealdorman of Mercia. Called *dux* on royal charters. *Maldon*, 218.

EALHHILD Daughter of Eadwine, King of the Lombards, wife of Eormanric the Goth. She gives Widsith a ring. Possibly to be identified with the Sunilda of Jordanes. See *Widsith*, 5 *n*.

EASTGOTA Ostrogotha, the founder of the Ostrogoths. Eormanric's great-great-grandfather. Mentioned at *Widsith*, 113, as one of Eormanric's followers and the father of Unwen.

EAST SAXONS The inhabitants of modern Essex. *Maldon*, 69.

EATS The Jutes, said by Bede to have come to Kent from Jutland, though scholars disagree. *Widsith*, 26.

EDGELEAVE Father of Ashferth. *Maldon*, 267.

EDWARD Bryhtnoth's bower-thane or chamberlain. *Maldon*, 117. The 'Long Edward' of l. 273 may be the same person.

EMERCA See *Widsith*, 112 *n*.

EORMANRIC The great king of the Ostrogoths, who in the third quarter of the fourth century ruled an empire that stretched from the Baltic to the Black Sea, according to Jordanes. Died 375. He was later credited with the murder of his son Frederick and his nephews the Herelings; also with the exiling of Dietrich von Bern (Theodoric the Ostrogoth). In legend he was a treacherous tyrant (*Widsith, Deor, Beowulf*). See *Widsith*, 9 *n*.

FIFELDOR An island at the mouth of the River Eider. See *Widsith*, 35 *n*.

FINN FOLCWALDING The lord of Finnsburgh, leader of the Frisians (*Widsith*, 27); not actually mentioned in *Finnsburgh*. His second name means 'folk-ruler's son'.

FINNSBURGH Finn's stronghold, the scene of *The Fight at Finnsburgh*. Its whereabouts in the Frisian islands are unknown. *Finnsburgh*, 36.

FRANKS The Germanic founders of France. *Widsith*, 24, 68.

FRIDLA See *Widsith*, 112 ff. *n*.

FRISIANS The inhabitants of the islands and marshes now drained to make the polders of Holland; Finn's people, *Widsith*, 27, 68. Traditionally a seafaring race. Gnomic Verses, 95.

GADD A kinsman of Offa. *Maldon*, 287.

GARULF A young Frisian who falls at Finnsburgh. Guthlaf's son. *Finnsburgh*, 18, 31.

GEATS (also Weather-Geats, Storm-Geats) Beowulf's people. They inhabited the area south of the lakes Wener and Wetter in southern Sweden. *Beowulf*, 224, 3137, 3153, 3178; *Widsith*, 58.

GIFECA Ruler of the Burgundians when they were neighbours of the Goths and Huns on the Vistula. *Widsith*, 19.

GISLHERE A Burgundian ancestor of Guthere mentioned at *Widsith*, 123, as one of the lords of Gothland.

GODRIC The loyal retainer of Bryhtnoth who fought till the end. Aethelgar's son. *Maldon*, 321.

GODRIC, GODWINE and GODWIY The three sons of Odda who fled the battlefield. *Maldon*, 187, 192, 237, 325.

GOTHS See Ostrogoths.

GRENDEL The monster who terrorizes Heorot, killed by Beowulf. A demon, sprung from the race of Cain. *Beowulf*, 195.

GUTHERE Gundahari, King of the Burgundians, who died in 436 in a famous last stand against the Huns. He is presented as a gold-giver at *Widsith*, 65–7 *n*.

GUTHERE A Frisian who tries to restrain Garulf at Finnsburgh. Possibly Garulf's uncle. *Finnsburgh*, 18.

GUTHLAF A follower of Hnaef at Finnsburgh. Sent by Hengest to gather help in Denmark. Possibly the Hunlafing of *Beowulf*. *Finnsburgh*, 16. The man mentioned at l. 33 may be a different person.

GUTHLAF Father of Garulf. *Finnsburgh*, 33.

HAGENA Hagen, leader of the Holm-Riggs or Island-Rugians, a tribe who lived in the German Baltic islands. See *Widsith*, 21–2 *n*.

HAMA A famous outlaw, mentioned with Widia at *Widsith*, 124, among the heroes of Gothland.

HEATHOBARDS A tribe who had a blood-feud with the Danes, possibly to be identified with the Heruli. See note on *Widsith*, 45 ff.

HENGEST Second-in-command of the Danes at Finnsburgh, he succeeds Hnaef as leader. Possibly the Hengest who invaded Kent. *Finnsburgh*, 17.

HEODEN Ruler of the Gloms, a tribe of the Baltic coast of Germany. See *Widsith*, 21–2 *n*. Founder of the Heodenings, Deor's tribe.

HEODENINGS The word means 'children of Heoden'. *Deor*, 36.

HEOROT Hrothgar's famous hall, the scene of the slaughter of the Heathobards. *Widsith*, 49; *Beowulf*, *passim*.

HEORRENDA Deor's successor as poet of the Heodenings. *Deor*, 39. See also *Widsith*, 21–2 *n*.

HERELINGS Eormanric's nephews, Emerca and Fridla, supposed to have been murdered by him at Sifeca's instigation. *Widsith*, 112.

HNAEF Leader of the Danes at Finnsburgh. *Finnsburgh*, 2, 40. He is called the son of Hoc in *Beowulf*, and at *Widsith*, 29, the ruler of the Hocings.

HOLM-RIGGS Island-Rugians. See Hagena.

HRETH-GOTHS See *Widsith*, 57 *n*.

HROTHGAR (modern Roger) King of the Danes, uncle of Hrothwulf, builder of Heorot. *Beowulf*, 235, 863. See note on *Widsith*, 45 ff.

HROTHWULF, HROTHULF (modern Ralph) Hrothgar's nephew, the famous Hrolf Kraki of Norse tradition. See note on *Widsith*, 45 ff.

HUNLAFING See Guthlaf.

HUNS Turkic peoples of the steppe. *Widsith*, 18.

HWALA Sceaf's grandson, according to the genealogy of the West Saxon royal house given in three versions of the *Anglo-Saxon Chronicle*. *Widsith*, 14.

HYGELAC King of the Geats, Beowulf's uncle. Mentioned in Gregory of Tours's *Historia Francorum* as having died in a raid on the Frisians, who at that time (*c.*521) formed part of the Merovingian Empire. The only character in *Beowulf* who is quite certainly historical. *Beowulf*, 194.

INGELD Chief of the Heathobards. See note on *Widsith*, 45 ff.

KAISER The emperor, either of the East (*Widsith*, 76) or of the West (*Widsith*, 20).

LEOFSUNU One of Bryhtnoth's men, from Sturmer, Essex. *Maldon*, 244.

LOMBARDS In the second century a tribe living between the Angles and the Swaefe on the north German coast, ruled by Sheaf (*Widsith*, 32). Under Aelfwine (Alboin) they invaded Italy in the sixth century. Also at *Widsith*, 80.

MACCUS The third defender of the *brycg* (*Maldon*, 80). The name indicates Norse descent.

MERCIANS The people of the English midlands. Allies of West Saxons at Brunanburgh. *Maldon*, 217.

MYRGINGS (also Broad-Myrgings) Widsith's people, identified in the poem with the Swaefe. They lived between the Eider and the Elbe. *Widsith*, 4, 23, 42, 84-5.

NITHHAD Father of Beadohild, enslaver of Wayland, as related in the first strophe of *Deor*.

ODDA Father of Godric, Godwine and Godwiy. *Maldon*, 186, 238.

OFFA The fourth-century founder of the Angles. See *Widsith*, 35 *n*.

OFFA King of Mercia in the eighth century. Builder of the Welsh dyke. See *Widsith*, 35 *n*.

OFFA Bryhtnoth's second-in-command, a kinsman of Gadd; he leads the English after his lord's death and the flight of Godric. *Maldon*, 5, 198, 230, 286, 288.

ONGENTHEOW King of the Swedes, often mentioned in *Beowulf*. *Deor*, 21; *Widsith*, 9 *n*, 31, 111.

ORDLAF A Dane, follower of Hnaef at Finnsburgh. See Guthlaf. *Finnsburgh*, 16.

OSTROGOTHS Eastern Goths. See under Eormanric.

OSWOLD Retainer of Bryhtnoth, brother of Eadwold. *Maldon*, 304.

PANTA, PANT The River Blackwater, which flows out to the sea below Maldon in Essex; still known by this name in the stretch below the town, according to E. Ekwall's *English River Names*.

ROME-WELSH Romans. 'Welsh' means 'foreign'. *Widsith*, 69, 78.

RUGIANS See Hagena.

SAEFERTH See Sigeferth.

SAXONS The inhabitants of the German North Sea coast who invaded southern England. *Widsith*, 62.

SCYLD Scyld Shefing, the founder of the Danish royal house; Hrothgar's great-grandfather. *Beowulf*, 26.

SCYLDINGS The children of Scyld; used of the Danes and of the Danish royal house. *Beowulf*, 30, 229.

SEAFOLA Mentioned with Theodoric the Ostrogoth as one of Eormanric's followers at *Widsith*, 115. The historical Sabene of Ravenna.

SECGAN See Sigeferth. *Finnsburgh*, 24; *Widsith*, 31.

SERINGS (?) Syrians. *Widsith*, 75.

SHEAFA Ruler of the Lombards ('Longbeards'), *Widsith*, 32. Mythical civilizer of the tribes of the North Sea coast, his name signifies the introduction of tillage. He stands at the head of the West Saxon genealogies. Under the name of Scyld Shefing, he is also the founder of the Danes.

SHILLING Widsith's fellow-*scop*. *Widsith*, 103.

SIBYRHT Retainer of Bryhtnoth, brother of Aetheric. *Maldon*, 282.

SIFECA A follower of Eormanric; in legend, the traitor who prompted Eormanric's murder of the Herelings. *Widsith*, 112 ff. *n*.

SIGEFERTH One of Hnaef's followers at *Finnsburgh*, 24; identical with the Saeferth who rules the Secgan at *Widsith*, 31.

SIGEMUND The great dragon-slayer. See *Beowulf*, 875 *n*.

SLIDING-FINNS A tribe who used snowshoes, probably Lapps. *Widsith*, 79.

SWAEFE Suevi, Suebi: a group of central German peoples. See under Myrgings. *Widsith*, 22, 44, 61.

SWEDES A tribe who inhabited only a small part of southern Sweden. *Widsith*, 31, 58.

THEODORIC Theodoric the Frank (*Widsith*, 24). The eldest son of Clovis, and himself king at Rheims from 511 to 534.

THEODORIC Theodoric the Ostrogoth, mentioned as one of Eormanric's retainers at *Widsith*, 115. Leader of the Ostrogothic nation into Italy, where they overcame Odoacer's Germans. Theodoric killed Odoacer in his palace at Ravenna on 15 March 493. He ruled from Verona for thirty years. In the *Nibelungenlied* he becomes the greatest knight, Dietrich von Bern. *Deor*, 18.

THURSTAN Father of Wistan. *Maldon*, 298.

VENDELS The inhabitants of modern Vendsyssel in Jutland; not the Vandals. *Widsith*, 59.

VIKINGS A general name for sea raiders, *Maldon*, *passim*; possibly a proper name at *Widsith*, 59.

WADA, WADE Ruler of the Hælsings. Originally a sea-giant. See *Widsith*, 21–2 *n*.

WAYLAND The Smith of Germanic legend. See *Deor*, 1 *n*.

WEST SAXONS The people of Wessex whose kings became rulers of a united England in the tenth century. The victors at Brunanburgh.

WIDIA The early Gothic champion Vidigioia, mentioned by the Latin historian Jordanes. In the lays he becomes the son of Wayland and Beadohild, and directly associated with Theodoric. At *Widsith*, 124 and 130, he and Hama are mentioned as the exiles who rule one of the peoples of Gothland.

WIDSITH The wandering poet of *Widsith*. Represented as a Myrging.

WIGELM Father of Offa. See *Maldon*, 300 *n*.

WISTAN Son of Thurstan, retainer of Bryhtnoth. *Maldon*, 297.

WULFMAER Son of Bryhtnoth's sister. *Maldon*, 113.

WULFMAER *SE GEONGA* (the Younger) The boy who stood at Bryhtnoth's side, not the same person as the above. *Maldon*, 155, 183.

WULFSTAN Son of Ceola, father of Wulfmaer *se geonga*. The Horatius of the *brycg* (*Maldon*, 75, 79, 155). The battle may have been fought on his land. See 75 *n*.